Relating to Voices using Compassion Focused Thera

Relating to Voices helps people who hear voices to develop a more compassionate understanding and relationship with them.

In this book, authors Charlie and Eleanor create a warm and caring tone for the reader and a respectful tone for their voices. With the help of regular "check-in boxes", the book guides the reader towards an understanding of what voices are, what they may represent, and how we can learn to work with them in a way that leads to a more peaceful relationship. It offers a shift away from viewing voices as the enemies, towards viewing them as potential allies in emotional problem-solving. This approach may be different to some others that readers have come across, which can often be about challenging voices, suppressing them, distracting from them, or getting rid of them. The Compassion Focused Therapy (CFT) approach suggests that we can learn to relate to both voices and ourselves in a way that is less about conflict and more about cooperation.

This book will be a useful companion for voice-hearers as well as for their supporters and allies in their journey of self-help. It will also be of use to mental health and social service workers.

Dr Charlie Heriot-Maitland is a clinical psychologist, researcher, and trainer at Balanced Minds, UK. For 13 years, Charlie provided psychological therapies in the UK NHS mental health services, and now offers a private CFT practice. He continues to provide supervision, training, and consultancy in the NHS, as well as other organisations across multiple sectors, including healthcare, social care, education, and charities.

Dr Eleanor Longden is a service-user research manager at the Psychosis Research Unit in Greater Manchester Mental Health NHS Foundation Trust (GMMH) in the UK, whose work draws upon her own experiences of recovery from trauma and psychosis. She is an honorary research fellow at the University of Manchester and co-director of GMMH's Complex Trauma and Resilience Unit.

Relating to Voices using Compassion Focused Therapy

A Self-help Companion

Charlie Heriot-Maitland and
Eleanor Longden

Routledge
Taylor & Francis Group

LONDON AND NEW YORK

Cover image: Getty

First published 2022
by Routledge
4 Park Square, Milton Park, Abingdon, Oxon OX14 4RN

and by Routledge
605 Third Avenue, New York, NY 10158

Routledge is an imprint of the Taylor & Francis Group, an informa business

British Library Cataloguing-in-Publication Data
A catalogue record for this book is available from the British Library

Library of Congress Cataloging-in-Publication Data
Names: Heriot-Maitland, Charlie, author. | Longden, Eleanor, author.
Title: Relating to voices using compassion focused therapy : a self-help companion / Charlie Heriot-Maitland and Eleanor Longden.
Description: Milton Park, Abingdon, Oxon ; New York, NY : Routledge, 2022. | Includes bibliographical references and index. |
Identifiers: LCCN 2021057898 (print) | LCCN 2021057899 (ebook) | ISBN 9780367762865 (hardback) | ISBN 9780367762841 (paperback) | ISBN 9781003166269 (ebook)
Subjects: LCSH: Emotion-focused therapy. | Compassion. | Voice.
Classification: LCC RC489.F62 C65 2021 (print) | LCC RC489.F62 (ebook) | DDC 616.89/14—dc23/eng/20211224
LC record available at https://lccn.loc.gov/2021057898
LC ebook record available at https://lccn.loc.gov/2021057899

ISBN: 978-0-367-76286-5 (hbk)
ISBN: 978-0-367-76284-1 (pbk)
ISBN: 978-1-003-16626-9 (ebk)

DOI: 10.4324/9781003166269

Typeset in Times New Roman
by Apex CoVantage, LLC

Contents

Foreword by Professor Paul Gilbert

I'm absolutely delighted to be able to write a foreword for this remarkable book on how to bring an evolutionary model of compassion to the experience of voice-hearing, which for some people can be so tormenting. Dr Eleanor Longden brings her wealth of experience of voice-hearing. She has been through very distressing experiences with voices, was prescribed medications, and at times was hospitalised before working out her own compassionate pathway of how to work with them. This is brilliantly discussed in her TED talk. Not only that, but she also went on to study for a PhD to better understand the psychology of voice-hearing and what can be helpful for other people. Dr Charlie Heriot Maitland, a colleague and clinical psychologist, became interested in compassion focused therapy (CFT) over 10 years ago when he saw the potential to apply it with those who experience serious mental health difficulties. He went on to complete his PhD investigating compassionate approaches to voice-hearing. Both are now regarded as international authorities on how to bring the motivational systems that underpin compassion to the experience of voice-hearing and the mental states associated with them.

CFT brings an evolution-informed, biopsychosocial model to the nature of our mind. One of the key insights that an evolution approach gives us is that so much of what goes on in us is *not of our design, not of our choice*, and *not our fault*. Another important insight is that our brain is highly evolved for social relating; indeed, it is sometimes called *a social brain*. CFT highlights the fact that evolved social motives, or what we call *social mentalities*, are used not only when we relate to other people, but also when we relate to ourselves. This means that we can sometimes treat ourselves as an object; for instance, we can like or dislike (parts of) ourselves, we can feel pride or shame in ourselves, and we can be sensitive to our own distress and think about how we can be helpful to ourselves. We can also be incredibly self-critical and literally *attack, condemn*, and *put ourselves down*. We can feel disappointed in ourselves and at times even hate ourselves. The big question, however, is: how do we experience or "hear" that kind of experience in our own heads? There is a way in which we can help people discover this for themselves using their imagination. We can invite people to think of something they are self-critical about and then to imagine their relationship with that critical part of themselves. We can start by inviting people to consider what their "critic" would look like if they could see it outside of themselves. People typically imagine dark shapes and hostile faces, or perhaps memories of real-life individuals who have been negative towards them. If we then ask people to focus on what their self-criticism *says*, it can often be quite aggressive and insulting. If we ask them to focus on the feelings their self-critical part has for them, it will typically be hostile or contemptuous; at the very least, quite unfriendly. And if we ask, "what does your self-critical part want to do to you?" then again this can usually be fairly hostile. As a reader, you may recognise this for yourself because it is a very common experience.

Crucial to this exercise is the recognition that while we can have streams of negative thoughts about a whole range of issues, when it comes to forms of self-criticism, these are commonly influenced by our direct social experiences. Therefore, we experience our internal relationship with ourselves as a flow of animated conversations which are sent and received between parts of ourselves – parts which can often have very different motivations, intentions, and emotions. Indeed, this is exactly how people describe it: "there is a part of me that is hostile and critical and another part of me that feels beaten down by it". Because this is an inner relationship, rooted in social experience, this is one of the reasons why switching that process into a different, more compassionate one is so important. We seek to change not just the content of thinking, but the motives and emotions of the inner conversations we have with ourselves. Indeed, for those of us who hear voices, our experience is not a stream of negative thoughts but an internal dialogue from a force which seems separate to us and has its own intentions and emotions. However, as we begin to understand that voice-hearing is not our fault, but instead a potential within our evolved human brain, it can help us to see our voices as influenced by things that have happened to us in our lives – and the importance of changing and developing our relationship with ourselves in a more compassionate way.

Another factor we should note about these processes is that they are very powerful *physically*. For example, consider how the types of relationships we focus on can have profound effects on our body and brain. Imagine lying in bed and going over an argument with somebody who really annoyed you and now you're planning how to get your own back. What happens in your body to your heart rate and blood pressure? How different would that be if you were imagining the excitement of going on holiday with friends tomorrow? You would have a totally different pattern of physical reactions in the body. The point to highlight here is that our imagined relationships and experiences are very powerful physically, and if we get caught up in a critical or hostile one then that is going to have profound effects in our brains and bodies. Indeed, we can even get trapped and stuck in these internally created conversations.

CFT suggests that we can learn to respond to both voices and ourselves in a way that is less about threat and domination and more based in compassion and care. In essence, compassion is our ability to be sensitive to distress and suffering and then find wise ways of helping. CFT therefore tries to help people become wisely sensitive to the nature of their suffering, and the nature of their voice-hearing, and how that might be linked to earlier experiences of a trauma or other negative events in the past. Whatever the source, the key is to recognise that we have got caught up in a negative, attacking way of responding to ourselves and our voices and therefore learn how to use compassion to wisely and courageously work with those voices. So, in CFT, we don't fight or rationalise with the voices, but instead seek to understand them and work with them, particularly the threat that sits behind them.

Charlie and Eleanor provide us with the first major overview of how to support voice-hearers by using this evolutionary-based model of switching mindsets from hostile and attacking towards compassionate and supportive. Early on, they highlight the key issue of being made to feel dominated or powerless. They provide an excellent guide into how to understand the general nature of voice-hearing as part of human experience. They guide readers into understanding that voices can have powerful effects in our body and that some voices can stimulate our sense of threat, while others can help us to feel safe.

There is a lot of confusion about compassion, particularly as it has become very popular on the internet. Eleanor and Charlie guide us through that complex area and help us recognise that compassion is not about love or kindness particularly, but instead a courageous sensitivity to want to engage with and address suffering – and that at the root of this is a motive for trying to reduce and prevent suffering wherever possible by using courage and wisdom.

Having laid down the basic map of the mind in Part 1, Part 2 guides us through the process of change. Again, a key understanding for this journey is the nature of our mind and how to use exercises in multiple ways to create physical changes that can help us feel safe(r), more grounded, and ultimately build a platform to help us find the courage to work with some of the more distressing and frightening aspects of our minds. They outline how we can develop different types of self-identities around different aspects of our mind. For example, we can have an identity as a parent, friend, or work colleague. However, we can also have aspects of ourselves that cluster around different emotions or motives: for example, we can experience ourselves as an angry self, an anxious self, a caring self, or a hating self. These are basically different patterns of activity in our brains. An important insight is that many of the brain states that cause us depression, anxiety, stress, or paranoia are not ones that we choose. Nobody wakes up in the morning and makes a decision to try and have a panic attack, or to be in a rage, or to become very depressed. These are mostly brain states we don't want. However, we can learn to cultivate brain states we *do* want, and which are helpful, by taking on certain types of identity and practising certain kinds of processes. We call this developing a Compassionate Self and mind. Again, Eleanor and Charlie guide us through with great skill and sensitivity in how to cultivate a Compassionate Self. This is the self that constantly tries to live using the compassionate motto: "to live to be helpful, not harmful, to myself and others". To help us, they have brought together a huge range of suggestions and exercises that will be of enormous value for people who are voice-hearers; indeed, for all of us actually.

As noted, compassion often requires courage and Part 3 is dedicated to helping us understand the nature of compassionate courage. Compassion can sometimes be seen as soothing and grounding, and while it is often both these things that is not always the case. For example, people who are firefighters are obviously highly compassionate because they are risking their lives to save others. However, they also won't be entering the burning house in a soothed state of mind. Instead, what is important is that they are able to regulate what might be very frightening emotions in order to pursue their intention to save people. Eleanor and Charlie point out that sometimes we also need courage to engage with our voices, particularly if they are hostile. Furthermore, we need to have the courage to see what might sit behind them; for example, sometimes there may be a lot of trauma that has caused our voices to appear. We might be required to explore that. Sometimes, we can become aware that perhaps we didn't receive the love and care that we wanted as children, and yet there's a part of us that still yearns for that. We may need to grieve for those losses and unmet needs in our life. We may have to deal with feelings of shame that we carry from the past. Both these things can require courage.

Ultimately CFT can help us see the emotional and physical value of deliberately cultivating compassion to help us when the contents of our mind can feel quite frightening and hostile. We constantly hold the principle that we didn't choose to have the minds we have; we didn't design them, and therefore, it's not our fault that we've got them. Once we let go of that and recognise that part of the courage of compassionate work is to try to bring some harmony to our minds rather than fight with them, we are more likely to be successful.

In this extremely far-reaching, encouraging, exciting, and insightful book, Charlie and Eleanor have succeeded in bringing many of the basic principles of compassion training based on years of careful study and personal and clinical experience, and used it to help us think about voices: how to work with them, how to have the courage not to be afraid of them, and how, instead of fighting with them, to instead gradually work towards ways of healing. One couldn't find better guides into this territory. Reading this book has been a heartening and fascinating experience for me personally and I hope for you too.

Professor Paul Gilbert OBE

Acknowledgements

We would like to thank all the many voice-hearers and colleagues whose wisdom and guidance over the years first inspired us to want to write this book. And thank you so much Wendy and Chris for proof-reading it before we were ready to share it with the world. Many thanks also to Paul, for giving us CFT.

Some suggestions for how to use this book

Welcome to our book! We are so glad to be spending this time together with you. We have a lot of information and ideas we'd like to share, but before we start, we'd like to take a moment to just notice the intentions that each of us has arriving here – both you as the reader of this book and we as the authors.

Your intention as a reader

This book has been planned as a form of "self-help". We know that's an obvious thing to say, but self-help is a phrase that gets used a lot; and when we hear a phrase over and over, it's sometimes easy to disconnect a bit from its meaning. So, let's just think for a minute about what this actually means: you are reading this book because you have chosen to do something to help <u>you</u>. Just hold that in mind for a minute. . . . So, you are arriving here, on page xii of this book, with the intention to do something helpful for yourself. That is a compassionate intention.

Our intention as authors

We (Charlie and Eleanor) have chosen to write this book because we want to help you. For most of our adult lives, we have been involved with various projects and jobs with the aim of helping voice-hearers. We are genuinely moved by the suffering and distress experienced by so many people, and we want to find ways to support them to struggle less with their voices and to lead happier and more peaceful lives. We were initially invited to write a book for professionals that work with voice-hearers, but our preference was to write this directly for you. So, both of us are also arriving here, on page xii of this book, with a compassionate intention towards you. We're glad to have you here, and are grateful that you have trusted us enough to listen to what we have to say and to let us share our ideas with you.

Using the check-in boxes

As we go through this book, we will be regularly checking in with you, your feelings, and your voices. We do this through what we call a "check-in box". The aim is to give you a chance to reflect on your own experience: for example, how you are reacting, and how your voices are reacting, to the various ideas and content you've just read. It is a bit like having an observer position as we go through, or what we have called a "view from the balcony". We hope that this observer view – a chance to take a step back and reflect on your experiences – becomes a useful place from which to take care of yourself. For instance, it may be important to remind yourself to take regular breaks. You might also consider keeping a diary of thoughts and feelings that come up as you're reading, and perhaps discuss it with a friend, family member, or a mental health worker. Each time you come across one of these boxes, it could be helpful to think in terms of these three steps:

1   Check in from the balcony.
2   How am I feeling? How are my voices feeling?
3   A reminder to take care of myself.

Later in the book, we expand the "check-in box" to include some of the skills and resources that we are learning along the way, especially skills around bringing compassion to yourself, your emotions, and your voices. So, towards the end of the book, we will be guiding you in how to check in with yourself, and how to show up compassionately for yourself. Here is an example of what these check-in boxes will look like:

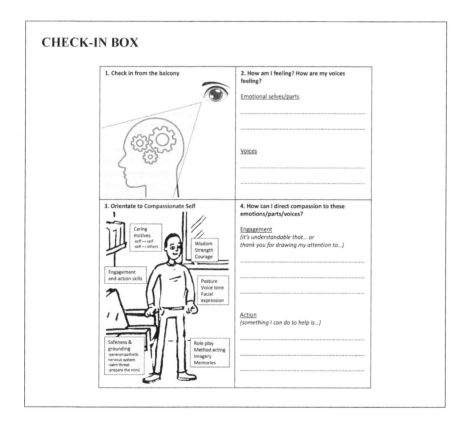

Using the practical boxes

There are a number of exercises in this book. These are presented in other boxes that we call a "practical box". One of the reasons we've included these is to give you the opportunity to have more of a hands-on understanding of the ideas we explore in the book. However, none of these are compulsory. The main learning points will be covered anyway in the text, so if you choose not to do an exercise then that's absolutely fine. The main thing is to take care of yourself. If it feels like the right time to do an exercise, and you think that it might be helpful, then please try it out. However, if it doesn't feel like the right time, then just skip it and carry on reading – and if you change your mind you can always make a note then come back to an exercise later at a time which feels more comfortable. In this respect, one way of thinking about this book is as a collection of invitations. The exercises are invitations to try things out if you would like to: for example, to try to think about things in a different way than you've perhaps had the opportunity to do before. However, you are the expert of your own experience, and your own wisdom about what feels useful or not is the most important guide. What we hope we can offer is some advice, support, and suggestions for you in finding what would be the most helpful way for you and your voices to move forward.

Some of the practical boxes contain exercises with invitations to close your eyes; for example, where we are using imagery techniques to create experiences of safeness and compassion. For exercises like this, we suggest that you either ask someone else to read the exercise to you, or you can record yourself reading the exercise first and then play it back. We have also put some recordings of us reading the exercises on a website we set up to accompany this book (www.relating tovoices.com). So, if you have access to the internet, you can play these directly from there. There may be other exercises that you might want to do together with another person such as a friend, a family member, or a trusted mental health professional. However, this is not essential, and they can all be done on your own too if you prefer.

One important recommendation, to help you get the most out of this book, is to read through all the sections in order. This is because we are gradually introducing you to ideas step by step. The ideas at the end of the book will build on ones discussed earlier.

Thank you for taking the time to read this introduction. Once again, we're grateful that you have chosen to let us try to support you and your voices, and we hope that the resulting journey together will be a useful and interesting one.

Part 1

Before we start

Chapter 1

Voice-hearing: A normal human experience

Chapter summary

So, what is voice-hearing?

In this chapter, we will be exploring some important questions about hearing voices, such as:

- Who hears voices?
- What kinds of voices do people hear?

We will then describe how voice-hearing can link to different emotions. In particular, we'll be focusing on three main groups of emotions which perform important jobs for us in our everyday lives:

- *The threat system:* emotions that focus on threat and protection.
- *The drive system:* emotions that focus on doing and achieving.
- *The soothing system:* emotions that focus on contentment and feeling safe.

Finally, we will set the scene for the work we're hoping to do together by sharing the personal accounts of five people who'll describe their own experience of bringing compassion into their relationship with their voices.

Introduction

It goes without saying that hearing voices which don't seem to be part of our own minds can be a distressing, frightening, and confusing experience. The natural thing to do when we are confronted with such difficult experiences is to try to get rid of them, but we may also wonder what it means about us. Does it mean we are crazy? Many people are told that they hear voices because they have a mental illness which is coming from abnormalities in the brain, and this can make them feel fearful and ashamed. However, if you hear voices, it's important to know that you have nothing to be ashamed of. Voice-hearing is a

DOI: 10.4324/9781003166269-2

normal human experience, shared by people of all ages, backgrounds, and cultures. One of us (Eleanor) has heard voices for over half her life, and the other (Charlie) has worked closely with voice-hearers for 15 years as a therapist. In turn, both of us have friends and work colleagues who hear voices and who live peaceful, successful lives.

For the last few years, the two of us have been working together in leading the development, training, and research of Compassion Focused Therapy (CFT) for voice-hearing, which is an approach that tries to help people learn to develop compassionate ways of relating with themselves and their voices. In this time, we have run numerous events and workshops in different countries, produced videos, and written articles. Our events have been attended by many voice-hearers, their friends and relatives, and the mental health professionals who support them. The reason we are writing this book is that we want to share some of the ideas and wisdom we have learnt over the years. What this book will do is help us understand what voices are, what they may represent, and how we can learn to work with them in a way that leads to a more peaceful relationship. Many people discover that when they understand their voices better, don't fight with them, and learn how to relate to them in a calmer and more confident way, they are able to live their lives with much less fear and a greater sense of contentment and joy.

The ideas and approaches in this book have emerged from the experiences of people who have suffered hugely because of distressing voices yet have gone on to cope successfully with them and to lead happy and fulfilling lives. For some of these people, their relationship with their voices changed so much that the voices became friends and allies. Some people tell us that they would actually miss their voices if the voices went away. Of course, you might be reading this thinking that this does not apply to you – that it seems so far away from the type of relationship or experience that you have with your voices as to be totally unrelatable. If so, that is a very understandable way to feel. We realise that there is such a wide range of different experiences with voices – an infinite range, in fact. It might be helpful just to keep in mind your own understanding of your voices, and to look after yourself while engaging with these ideas. The same applies to your voices, who may also find that this does not apply to them, or perhaps have some reaction to what we are telling you. If so, bring the voices in. For example, if a voice is telling you not to read the book, ask what is it worried about? Is there anything that would help it feel less threatened? Perhaps, you could remind the voice that one of the authors is a voice-hearer herself. After speaking with many voice-hearers, we also find it is not uncommon for voices to feel frustrated with being in a negative, argumentative relationship with the person who hears them, so maybe it would be helpful to remind them that there may be benefits for them too if you read this book. Whatever you decide, look after yourself and your voices by considering what you need to feel safe in this moment.

Who hears voices?

The short answer is that, given the right circumstances, any human being is capable of hearing voices. Despite what you may have been told, voice-hearing in itself is not a mental illness, and voices are not only heard by people in mental health services. Nor is it true that only people with a diagnosis of schizophrenia hear voices, because it can occur in a wide range of different diagnoses – everything from depression to posttraumatic stress. However, what's also important to know is that many people who hear voices have never used mental health services at all – and are not only untroubled by their voices, but actively find them to be a helpful and enriching presence in their lives. In fact, there is considerable evidence that a wide range of voice-hearing experiences exist throughout the whole population, which can vary from just occasionally hearing a voice saying one or two words, to hearing many voices constantly [1]. It is estimated that around 12% of children hear voices (often in the form of imaginary friends), and for adults the figure is somewhere between 5 and 15%. A number of famous and noteworthy people have spoken and written about their experiences with hearing voices. These include well-known actors (e.g. Anthony Hopkins and Zoe Wannamaker), musicians (e.g. John Frusciante of the Red Hot Chili Peppers, Lady Gaga, the dubstep artist Benga, and Danny McNamara from the band Embrace), sportspeople (e.g. Zinedine Zidane and Vinnie Jones), and famous historical figures (Gandhi, Joan of Arc, and Sigmund Freud).

In this respect, it is increasingly clear that the presence of voices isn't so much of a problem as the *type of relationship* we have with our voices. In other words, someone who feels very distressed by their voices is far more likely to struggle with them; and this, in turn, is more likely to happen when the person is also experiencing other difficulties in their lives. For example, this might include:

- feeling depressed and/or anxious
- being very isolated
- not having helpful coping strategies
- using drugs or alcohol
- being a survivor of trauma or abuse

If you recognise any of your own experiences in this list, remember that this is not your fault, and you are *not* responsible for the distress you feel from your voices. Instead, it is likely that certain difficulties in your life have come together to make you feel overwhelmed, and that's something we really hope we can help you with in this book.

What kinds of voices do people hear?

Just like people, no two voices are the same. Some voice-hearers find their experience a source of support, companionship, or helpful advice; for instance, the voices may arrive following a loss or bereavement and be very comforting. For example, according to one study in Sweden, 30% of people were still hearing the voice of their partner a month after they had died [2]. However, for some people, voice-hearing can be an extremely negative event. This can be because voices are very upsetting, because people around us may not understand or make us feel ashamed of these experiences, or it could be a combination of both these things. Sometimes voices can sound like people we know, or have known, in our life, or they can say things that are so cruel, unpleasant, or disturbing that it feels impossible that our minds could ever create such statements. This is a very understandable way to feel and can make it seem that the voices could only be coming from outside of ourselves. Everyone is of course their own expert about their experience, and we are not claiming that we know more about your voices than you do yourself. However, in this book, we would like to explore some possible suggestions for why we think voices can sometimes say things that feel so terrible and cruel, and why they can seem so at odds with how our own minds would think. We will come back to this in the next section when we talk about voice-hearing and emotions, particularly emotions related to a feeling of threat.

CHECK-IN BOX

How are you feeling reading about this? Do you need to take a break? Would it be helpful to talk about how you are feeling, or write down a couple of things? It may be that your voices have become angry or upset, in which case we would like to reassure them that it is not our intention to make them feel this way. Some people find it helpful to explore different ways of understanding their experiences, but there is no pressure for you or your voices to agree with what we are saying. If you feel something doesn't apply to you that is fine. There is still a lot to come in the book that you might find helpful.

In order to give you a sense of the range of voice-hearing experiences that occur across different groups of people, we would like to share with you some research that one of us (Charlie) did, which was published in the *British Journal of Clinical Psychology* in 2012 [3]. We interviewed 12 people about their personal "out-of-the-ordinary" experiences, all of which had started within the last five years. Six of them were recruited from mental health services (the "clinical group"), and six from the wider population with no mental health service involvement (the "non-clinical group"). The majority of the experiences they reported were hearing voices and receiving messages from sources outside their own mind. The presence of these experiences was similar between both groups (see table below). However, the *way* they were described was very different. For the clinical group, the experiences were all talked about in medical terms, such as "symptoms" of a psychotic illness, but for the non-clinical group, they were not symptoms, but rather described in terms of spiritual/religious experiences, or as psychic abilities or mediumship skills.

A brief description of people's experiences in both the clinical and non-clinical groups.

Participant	Out-of-the-ordinary experience (OOE)	Group
Holly	Receiving visions from God	
Omar	Body taken over by spirits	
Beth	Telepathic communication and speaking with God	Clinical
Tom	Receiving symbolic messages from other realms	
Nessa	Hearing voices, and thoughts of being watched/filmed	
Leroy	Hearing voices when nobody is there	
Jenny	Body taken over by spiritual energy	
Clive	Visions of people who have died and religious figures	
Maria	Receiving words directly from God	Non-clinical
Daniel	Spiritual calling, and developing intuitive perception	
Flora	Visions and voices of spirits (mediumship skills)	
Stefan	Body taken over by an external force	

Table adapted from Heriot-Maitland, Knight & Peters (2012) [3]

The main aim of this study was to compare experiences between these two groups of participants, and to try and understand what factors might influence why some people who have such experiences need mental health support while others don't. The findings showed that there were indeed a lot of similarities between the two groups. Not only were they both experiencing similar things, but they also both started experiencing them during a period of significant negative emotion. In turn, their experiences were generally meaningful and relevant to these emotional concerns. However, one thing that was very different between the groups was their social experiences, particularly in terms of whether they had received accepting and supportive responses from others around them. By now, you will probably not be surprised to know that the non-clinical group had received much more acceptance and support than the clinical group. This is an important finding, and we will discuss it in more detail in the following section when we think about the connection between voice-hearing and emotions.

Hearing voices in an emotional and social context

In the Compassion Focused Therapy (CFT) approach to improving our well-being, we find it helpful to try to understand our emotions in terms of their function. What is the job of this emotion? Why have humans evolved emotions? What is this emotion doing for us, or helping us with? And as we will see through the pages of this book, we can also start to think about voices and voice-hearing in a similar way. What is the job of this voice-hearing experience? Why have humans evolved voice-hearing as a capability? What is this voice-hearing doing for us or helping us with?

In CFT, we use an idea called the "three-system model" (also called the "three-circle model" because, as you'll see from the following, we usually draw it out as circles) [4]. This approach groups emotions in terms of their different functions and describes three major emotion systems:

(1) **Threat system** – the function of these emotions is detecting threat and avoiding harm. The threat system emotions (such as anger, anxiety, and disgust) help us to take actions to protect ourselves from bad things happening.

(2) **Drive system** – the function of these emotions is seeking out things that we want or need, and the drive system emotions (such as joy, excitement, and pleasure) help us to take actions that are necessary to obtain resources, rewards, and other things that are important to us. This could be anything from food and shelter to a promotion at work, to getting the newest game console or concert tickets.

(3) **Soothing system** – the function of these emotions is rest and relaxation. The soothing system emotions (such as peacefulness and contentment) help us to settle, rest, and recuperate, particularly in the moments when we are not focused on the other two sets of emotions. The soothing system has also become linked with social experiences of caring, attachment, and bonding, in that its calming responses can arise through experiences of social safeness and connection.

PRACTICAL BOX

EXERCISE: Your three emotion systems

In this exercise, we would like to invite you on a journey of getting to know your own three emotional systems. This will then help us to start thinking about where your own voice-hearing experiences might sit in relation to them. We briefly introduced threat, drive, and soothing earlier, but we want to add a bit more detail now so that you can start to get more of a *feel* for what these systems are like when we experience them in the body.

Your threat system

Suppose that you heard a sound in your kitchen late at night. What might go through your mind? What might happen in your body? What other sorts of things make you anxious?

Imagine being in one of those situations. What does your body feel like? What do you pay attention to? What do you think about? How do you behave?

. . . .

. . . .

Your drive system

Suppose that you just found out that you've won the lottery jackpot. What might happen in your body? What might go through your mind? What kind of things give you joy?

Imagine being in one of those situations. What does your body feel like? What do you pay attention to? What do you think about? How do you behave?

. . . .

. . . .

Your soothing system

For some of us, it may be that experiences of feeling safe and soothed are more difficult to relate to than the others, so we might need to use our imagination about this one. What do you imagine your body would feel like if you were content, or if others were being kind to you? What about if you felt kindness for yourself? If you did feel safe and content, what sort of things would you pay attention to and think about? How would you behave?

. . . .

. . . .

Great – thank you for trying this exercise. We hope this gives you a deeper sense of what we mean by the three systems. Don't worry if you didn't get much of a *felt* experience of one (or more) of these. There will be plenty of opportunities to come back to this in later chapters.

Throughout the book, we will often be referring back to these three systems. As you will see, the three-system model will provide a useful way of understanding the role our emotions have in voice-hearing, as well as giving us a roadmap for how we might use emotion to help improve our relationship with voices. In this diagram, the three systems are represented as three shaded circles: threat (grey), drive (white), and soothing (black). In colour-printed publications, these three systems are normally illustrated in three colours: threat (red), drive (blue), and soothing (green), which is helpful to know if you would like to cross-refer to other books and articles on this subject.

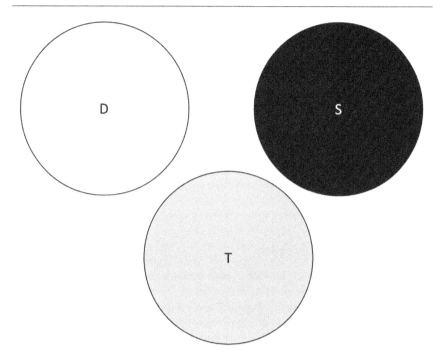

The three circles

These three emotion systems are universal, and every human being has them. Although some emotions are more pleasant than others, they are all likely to have evolved over time to be helpful to us in some way or another. Thinking in terms of these three main emotion systems can offer a useful framework for exploring how our brain creates different feelings, desires, and urges. It can also give us a framework for exploring the different kinds of voices that we hear. Just like emotions, some voices might be linked to the threat system, some to the drive system, and some to the soothing system.

In the example we gave earlier about the comforting voices heard by grieving people, what system does that sound like? To us, it sounds a bit like soothing. Perhaps these voices are providing a connection that creates calming and peacefulness after a loss. Or for some people, it could be a bit more drive-based, in that the voice creates guidance and direction to go out into the world. One of us (Charlie) used to work with a young voice-hearer, "Alex", who lost his father at the age of 13. As a boy entering his teenage years, an important source of direction and guidance in his life had suddenly been taken away, and he was not emotionally ready for the new role that was expected of him (as "the man of the house"). Alex started hearing the voice of his father, which provided the direction and advice that he needed. He listened to this guidance and welcomed it. It was comforting and encouraging to hear the voice and, in time, it became a motivator to help him to go out to explore the world and achieve things. In terms of the three emotion systems, it sounded as though the voice might have had some functions linked to soothing (as in comfort and companionship) as well as some linked to drive (as in encouragement and direction to explore, when otherwise he might have felt vulnerable and lost).

Interestingly, as Alex grew up and started taking his final school exams aged 18, the voices became louder and more critical. The extra stress and pressure created by the exams meant that his threat system was more activated – and the voices, in turn, became more linked to the threat system. It was at this point that his underlying fears became the main force in shaping his experiences with, and relationship to, his voices. For this young man, the voices seemed to go through stages of being linked to each of his three emotion systems – first soothing, then drive, and then threat. It was in the final stage (the "threat" stage) when he came to seek support from mental health services.

In the research study described earlier, with groups of people who did and did not need mental healthcare, we also heard many examples of positive and excited feelings that came with their experiences. Maria, who heard a voice she believed to be God, said she was "feeling it in my body, and it was giving me a lot of joy". Holly said that she felt a "really profound sense of love . . . deeper and more magnificent than anything else I'd ever felt", and Clive said "I got this terrific warm feeling, this very warm, loving feeling, and it was amazing. And I wanted it to go on. I didn't want it to stop". Beth said that her voice provided her with "company", explaining that "God saw my suffering and he wanted to use me . . . to help me, you know, yeah, that's why he gave me a guardian, which is the voice". Again, we can detect some aspects of the drive system (joyfulness) coming through in these experiences, as well as some aspects around calming/soothing of distress.

Generally, the kinds of voices that people hear in mental health settings are voices that are strongly linked to the threat system. Sometimes the threat can be from the content of what the voices are saying: for example, the voice is being aggressive, or making critical, shaming remarks about the voice-hearer (we will go into much greater detail about the different types of voices, and threat-based relationships with voices, in Chapter 6). However, at other times, it may be that the threat is more from the social experiences a voice-hearer has with other people. This social aspect is very important and was actually one of the major findings to come out of the study we described earlier. You may remember that while the voice-hearing and out-of-the-ordinary experiences were fairly similar in both groups, there were dramatic differences between the two groups in their social experiences with other people; specifically, many more voice-hearers in the non-clinical group received supportive responses from others (5, compared to 1 person in the clinical group), and many more of the clinical group received unhelpful or negative responses (5, compared to 1 in the non-clinical group).

So, could it be at *this* stage – the stage where we share our experience with other people – where some people's voice-hearing becomes linked to threat? Is it this *social* stage, when we talk to others about our voices and hear their response, that switches the threat system on or off? One of us (Eleanor) gave a TED talk in 2013, where she described how her friend's negative reaction to being told about her voice felt like a key moment in changing her own view of it from something she'd seen as relatively harmless – and at times, even quite reassuring – into something far more sinister and disturbing. Sometime later, she did an interview with a journalist about voice-hearing, and he referred to this moment in quite an interesting way. He said, "It seems like it wasn't so much of a problem until people started telling you it was", and in the years since she has met many other voice-hearers with similar stories. For example, "David" heard voices from a very young age and referred to them as being his best friends. However, in his early 20s, he became involved in a religious community who told him the voices were signs of demonic possession. His response to the voices immediately became more negative; and as soon as that happened, then the voices changed towards him too, and started speaking to him in a much more aggressive and hostile way.

It makes a lot of sense that the fear which comes from such social interactions (including many later experiences with mental health professionals) could cause voices to become more linked with the threat system. What if our social experiences at that time had been different? What if the people we told about our voices had been calm and supportive, then gave us the space to sit down, listen, and talk through what was happening? Of course, we can't ever say for sure (and it's important to remember that some of us hear voices which never felt soothing and appeared threatening from the very start). But certainly, in the research study, there are quotes from participants that really highlight the big emotional difference between a social encounter about voice-hearing that is supportive and accepting, compared to one that is unsupportive and rejecting:

> [I] relayed this experience to psychiatrists in the [hospital] and was sent for EEG tests, was told that I was hallucinating, was, this guy just didn't listen to, just obviously hadn't heard anything really that I'd said. . . . I just felt that this really positive experience was just scrutinised and just not, just like mocked. I didn't feel offended, I just thought they were being really stupid, and disregarding this kind of, yeah, really important thing.
>
> (Holly)

> Somebody came up to me and said "well, you know, we really need to hear from you. That's a very powerful message to people, and they need to hear that message". And that did matter to me.
>
> (Clive)

> I needed affirmation, that's what I needed, er, to help me contextualise it and make sense of it. . . . I suppose I did need kind of affirmation from other people that it was all ok.
>
> (Daniel)

In terms of CFT's three-system model (threat, drive, and soothing), these different social experiences are likely to play a big role in switching different emotional responses on or off. Our threat system is designed by evolution to be highly sensitive to social experiences of fear, exclusion, inferiority, and rejection, and if these are what we encounter socially, then of course it's our threat system that will be switched on. In turn, what this also means is that all the processes and mindsets associated with the threat system will be switched on too and are going to have a major impact on what we think, how we feel, the way we act, and the types of things we pay attention to. There is nothing "wrong" or "unnatural" about this; it is simply our brain working as it should. The threat system is doing its job, which is to protect us from harm. However, if our social experiences include things such as listening, connection, kindness, and a sense of safeness, then very different sorts of emotions and mindsets will be switched on instead. We will explore these ideas in a little more detail later in the book. However, for now, it is important to know that our social experiences (for example, ones which are either threatening or reassuring) may not only influence the *type of relationship* we have with our voices, but also the *type of voices* we hear.

As you have probably guessed, both of us (Charlie and Eleanor) strongly believe that the social context of voice-hearing is crucial. A lot of our work is about how to help voice-hearers experience accepting, non-shaming, and compassionate relationships with others, and ultimately with themselves. This focus on relationships comes from both our personal experiences, from the accounts of other voice-hearers, and from scientific research, particularly on how social experiences influence our emotions and our brains. This is also one of the main reasons why we are both big supporters of the Hearing Voices Movement, which is a leading movement across the world that aims to create validating, supportive social spaces for voice-hearers. The Hearing Voices Movement was established in 1987 in the Netherlands by Professor Marius Romme and Dr Sandra Escher alongside numerous voice-hearers who collaborated with them. Soon after, in 1988, the first UK hearing voices peer-support groups began to be run, and the movement has grown rapidly ever since, with 35 national networks and hundreds of hearing voices groups running all over the world by 2015.

One of us (Eleanor) has been fortunate enough to be involved with Intervoice (the organising body for the international Hearing Voices Movement), and has also done some research into the benefits of attending hearing voices groups, which explored how they can: create safe, accepting spaces to share experiences of voice-hearing; provide opportunities to develop a positive identity as someone who hears voices; and discuss strategies around the relationship with, and impact of, the voices people hear [5]. There are also some wonderful anti-stigma campaigns which aim to improve acceptance and understanding of voice-hearing experiences among the general public. One notable campaign we would like to mention is the Only Us campaign, which calls for an end to the type of "them and us" messages that divide people into those who have mental health issues and those who do not. The campaign points out that we are all on a range of different experiences when it comes to mental health: "There is no them and us. There's only us". In the Appendices, we have included details of how to get in touch with organisations like the Hearing Voices Movement that can help to create a sense of social safeness, acceptance, and peer-support around voice-hearing experiences.

The threat system and voice-hearing

As we mentioned earlier, most of the voice-hearing experiences which are distressing for people are linked to the threat system – the system that has evolved to detect and respond to danger. One of the ways in which our threat system keeps us safe is to notice when social encounters involve *threat-giving* (when we meet someone we see as more powerful than us) and *threat-receiving* (when we feel we are in a more vulnerable or helpless position than the other person). As we will explain in more detail in Chapter 2, our minds are very quick to notice these kinds of social roles and require immediate action to try and protect us from possible harm. To do this, we have evolved patterns in our mind that get switched on; so, in this case, it would be the "*threat-giving – threat-receiving*" mindset (which researchers sometimes call "*dominant-subordinate*"). These mindsets or mentalities are built into our brains through evolution to organise our relationships. They help us to instantly identify social roles in others and to switch into our own social roles and responses. As we go through this book, we will discover that another important mindset is the *care-giving – care-receiving* mindset, which is built in to organise other relationships – those that involve caring and attachment.

It is important to know that the threat system (and the *threat-giving – threat-receiving* mindset) is far more likely to be switched on for those of us who have experienced harm from others in the past. So, for example, if we have experienced bullying, discrimination, or abuse, then our threat system will have learned that this is what to expect about our environment. This is a very understandable response, and it means that our threat system is going to be working extremely hard to try and predict further sources of harm in future. It will be scanning our environment to check for threats, focusing our attention on possible danger and, if it doesn't find anything, it will probably "fill in the gaps" by making us imagine scary things that *might* happen. However, while this process can make us feel distressed, that isn't the intent of the threat system. It doesn't even notice it. All our threat system cares about is how to protect us and keep us as safe as possible. It doesn't pay attention to whether or not we feel happy, but it *does* care about whether or not we are safe – and it will do whatever it thinks is necessary to make sure this happens.

When we think about voice-hearing being linked to the threat system, we might therefore ask ourselves the question: "what is the *protective* job of this voice-hearing experience?" To answer this, we might consider functions for both detecting threats and responding to threats. For example, for threat-detection, we might ask "is this voice drawing my attention towards a potential danger?" For threat-response, we might ask "Is this voice helping me to avoid or to manage a problem?" With this question, we might be better off looking at what response the voice is creating in us. For example, is it making us want to withdraw and hide ourselves away from other people? Or is it encouraging us to always give into their demands and put their needs before our own? Whatever the case may be, it can be helpful to ask ourselves why the voice is creating this particular response in us. Another thing we could consider is what the voice might be drawing our attention *away* from. For example, is the voice's comments and behaviour distracting us from things like painful memories and emotions that could make us feel overwhelmed and helpless if we allowed ourselves to notice them? All of these possibilities for threat-based functions of voices will be explored in detail in Chapter 6.

One other important thing to know about the threat system is that it is very good at "self-monitoring". Self-monitoring means doing things like checking for errors or problems, detecting them, then drawing our attention to them, and the threat system is exceptional at it. Remember that its job is to help us avoid harm, and to do that job well sometimes means that the threat system needs to be forceful in drawing our attention to something. Of course, this needs to be most powerful of all when our survival is most at stake. Remember, as we described before, the threat system is not interested in our happiness; its only interest is in our survival (*it's better to be safe than sorry* is the threat system's favourite motto). So, if the most effective way of helping us survive is to shout and swear and scream the loudest, then that is what the threat system will do. It might grab our attention with hostile, critical comments and, of course, the things that will grab our attention the most are the words and phrases that we are the most sensitive to. These words and phrases are the most effective ways of creating a protective response in us. It's a bit like how children bully other children at school – they go straight in for the crudest, most direct insult as the best way of "getting a response".

CHECK-IN BOX

How are you feeling reading about this? This might be different to some of the ways you've heard people talk about voices and voice-hearing in the past. When we talk about voices as "protective" or "doing a job for us", it might seem contradictory to you and to your own experience with voices. This is very understandable. Of course, by suggesting that voice-hearing is linked to the threat system, and has a protective function, this is in no way suggesting that voice-hearing doesn't cause enormous suffering and distress for people. It can and it does. So, let's just see if we can explain why this contradiction exists – why something that can be so distressing to us in our lives can also be understood as trying to achieve something helpful for us.

By linking voice-hearing to the threat system, all we are saying is that its main focus is on keeping us safe. Over many millions of years of evolution, threat-protection (and therefore the survival of our genes) is perhaps the most powerful life task that humans have. Remember, our threat system is not concerned with whether or not we are feeling happy and peaceful in our lives. It is blunt, direct, and rapid, and it only cares about "better safe than sorry".

To summarise, the suggestion here is that hearing voices can be a way of rapidly and effectively "switching on" the threat system and producing responses in us that have been protective in the past (such as avoiding or mistrusting other people, dissociating, and checking for threats). Of course, the voices can also cause us further distress and we can end up feeling defeated or anxious because of the things they say. However, the outcome *overall* is that we are more likely to avoid the harm, or potential harm, from other people.

If you have concerns or disagreements about what you've just read, perhaps you can write them down and discuss them with someone you trust? And again, don't worry if you or your voices feel these ideas don't relate to you. That's fine, and there's nothing wrong with disagreeing with us. For now, all we would ask is that you keep them in mind as something to come back to later. In the meantime, if you don't want to use your voices as an example of the threat system protecting you, then perhaps you can read the rest of the chapter by thinking about your emotions instead, such as fear or worry.

How are your three systems balanced?

Earlier on we showed you a simple diagram of the three circles, using three different shades for each circle: threat (grey), drive (white), and soothing (black). One of the helpful things about having this kind of image is that we can use it to track how active each system is being. Specifically, the circles can be drawn with different sizes to illustrate how each of the three systems is balanced with each other in any particular situation. In the following example, we can see that the first image shows someone whose threat system is very active with hardly any soothing going on. Their drive system is a little larger, so perhaps this person is about to do a task that feels scary, like taking an exam.

In the second, we can see that the drive system has taken over, and the sense of threat and sense of soothing are balancing each other out. Perhaps this person has just had some good news; for example, they passed their exam with the grades they needed. They don't feel threatened, but they are also too excited to feel relaxed.

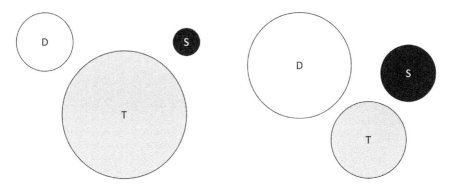

How are the three circles balanced?

Over time, you might start to develop more awareness of how the emotion systems actually *feel* for you as physical sensations in your body. You might also start to notice how the activity, "sizes", and balance of your emotion systems may be linked to certain situations (such as social experiences), and to your interactions with your voices. You might notice how certain emotions are linked to certain thinking styles and ways of paying attention, such as imagining the worst outcome. You might also notice that your voices can sometimes change as the balance of the emotion systems changes. We'll explore this in more detail in Chapter 3. The main point for now is that these three emotion systems are built into all of us. We all have the hardwiring for these systems, and although we differ in how each of them has been activated in our past (for instance, during childhood) and how they influence us day-to-day, we can still learn to notice, experience, and track them as we go through our lives. To help us begin to notice our own three emotion systems, we would like to invite you to have a go at the exercise in the practical box, which considers how they might be balanced in three different situations: 1) in day-to-day life; 2) in a social situation, and 3) in your relationship with a voice.

PRACTICAL BOX

EXERCISE: How are your three circles balanced in each of these situations?

Typically, in your day-to-day life

(think about this for minute, and if you like, draw the sizes of each circle in this space)

In a particular social situation

For example, when you were last with someone you know. This could be someone you like or someone who makes you feel intimidated – whatever feels most relevant.

(think about this for minute, and if you like, draw the sizes of each circle in this space)

In your relationship with a particular voice

(think about this for minute, and if you like, draw the sizes of each circle in this space)

Thank you for doing that. Remember that we can track these three systems across any situation: for example, we can ask ourselves "how are my three systems balanced?" in a particular relationship (e.g. with a family member, mental health worker, or voice), a particular place (e.g. when I go shopping, or when I'm in a crowd), or at a particular time (e.g. right now, or when I was at work).

Switching from "threat mind" to "compassionate mind"

Earlier in this chapter we described the example of Alex, whose voice-hearing experiences seemed to switch between different emotion systems over a few years; in his case, from soothing, to drive, and to threat. We also described a number of examples where voices seemed to start off as quite comforting and fulfilling, but then switched into threat through difficult social experiences when people's reactions made the voice-hearer feel rejected and ashamed. This invites us to consider the idea of "pattern switching" more generally. For example, if distressing voices are linked to the threat system, then what if we could intentionally switch the emotion system from "threat" to "safeness"? What if we could intentionally switch our mindset from "threat-giving – threat-receiving" to "caregiving – care-receiving"? Would this kind of switching change the experience of voice-hearing?

Well, we both ourselves have certainly experienced the benefits of switching on compassion in our personal lives. One of us (Eleanor) has talked about this already in her TED talk [6]. But please don't just take our word for it. There are a number of other voice-hearers who have also tried this out for themselves and have written about their experiences of bringing compassion into their relationships with their voices. Here are the personal accounts of five inspiring people who have done just that (Jacqui Dillon, Indigo Daya, Mark Ellerby, Gerrard Russell, and Valerie Levey). We are very grateful to each of them for sharing their personal experiences to guide our own learning and also, we hope, to help others like you, the readers of our book. We will now leave you with their own words to finish this first chapter.

Jacqui Dillon

My voices were more than just voices. They were different selves.

Rather than trying to eradicate these different parts of me I tried to transform my relationship with them. Each was part of the whole of me. I learnt that I needed to listen to them and understand them and the context in which they had emerged – and to greet them with compassion and understanding. I began to honour them as they had helped me to survive. We each worked towards supporting and understanding each other, which increased our sense of connectedness and wholeness. Over time, life has become a shared, mutual collaboration. Gradually I felt less ashamed about who I was and began to marvel at how creative I had been in surviving such monstrous abuse. I became excited by what my mind had managed to invent. At times it felt like I had created a work of art.

Jacqui Dillion [7]

Indigo Daya

So, the Judge would say something like, "filthy whore, you have to die". And then Mrs Ingalls would say, "My darling Indigo, these are very hard words, and I don't believe them and I won't use them. We all have goodness in us. You must live, and focus on your goodness".

In a way it did help me get discharged, even though no-one else knew it. Because it helped me to start relating to the Judge in a wholly different, and kinder way. Creating an internal Mrs Ingalls awakened the compassionate part of myself. It didn't stop the Judge. It didn't change the content of what he said, or how he said it. But it began to change how I felt about what the Judge said. It began to change my responses, too.

I began to visualize the Judge as an angry, screaming baby in distress. And I would hold my hand to forehead, the way that a mother does to a sick child, the way that Mrs Ingalls would, and whisper to the Judge, "I love you, I hear you, I know you are hurting, I know you only want me to be good".

Indigo Daya [8]

Mark Ellerby

I am still developing my compassionate image. I have to imagine myself at my most non-judgemental, warm, resilient, courageous and wise. Then I have been using this mindset to address my critical voices. I have begun to understand and talk to them from this perspective. This approach is encouraging me to see the function of the voices, to see that I can have a different relationship with them, to know that I don't have to "prove" myself to them. Instead I may be able to see them as misguided attempts to guide me but not as true facts! It will be interesting to see how much I can develop a compassionate dialogue with them.

Mark Ellerby [9]

Gerrard Russell

I realised that being at war with the voices was the completely wrong thing for me to be doing. I was actually making war with myself. I was fighting my own consciousness; a self-defeating arrangement. This Compassionate Therapy taught me to soothe these voices if they came back, and also that it was important for me to try to find the source and the cause of these voices. I could not find any reason for them so I went through my life experiences and forgave every person in every scenario I could find in my memories. I also forgave myself of any blame for any actions I may have taken in the past that might have harmed anyone. I was defragmenting my brain, trying to reset it, and it has worked!

Gerrard Russell [10]

Valerie Levey

Previously, my voices would've been angry, threatening and controlling, with brittle and nasty tones. However, I applied compassionate well-being for myself by grounding myself, then self-soothing and finally using imaging. I also soothed the voices. During this practice from therapy, I felt a little calmer and also experienced a strong compassion towards myself, the voices and others. The voices response was to soften their tone and then become quiet. This is both a massive breakthrough and a learning curve.

Long ago I was told the voices were demonic, which meant they could act with cunning sophistication. I evolved out of believing in any spirits though. In CFT I've been invited to adopt an open and understanding mind to get to know the voices better. What I discovered is that these portals to my inner world are unsophisticated, with a very limited vocabulary and repetitive themes. The therapist suggested focusing on the tone rather than the content of the voices. What I discovered in amongst the surface nasty, brittle tone was a core of pain and hurt. While the therapist and I continued to dialogue with authentic compassion and curiosity towards the voices, the tone of the voices becomes soft, warm and gentle. But still the hurt and pain remains at their core. It is such a relief, for the voices to become kinder in their tone. A few times, the voices dispersed when I applied compassionate sensitivity. When that happened for the first time, I felt a mixture of relief and joy. However, in CFT, I'm also applying courageously some new solutions to live collaboratively alongside these hurting fragmentations that are the voices.

When the voices threaten I'm passing-on cancer and/or insanity to people, I use techniques that have been helpful in my therapy sessions. One of them is to firstly ground myself, access my Compassionate Self and then firmly but kindly reassure and soothe the voices that all is well.

I have noticed since working with compassionate well-being for myself and the voices that my on-going depression is less deep. I sometimes feel a lightness I've not enjoyed in decades. I'm reluctant to presume this is permanent though.

The therapist has invited me to respond to difficult emotions (such as fear and anxiety) that the voices try to protect me from, by applying compassionate qualities to them. This involves accessing my compassionate understanding and wisdom, while allowing the feeling to simply be what it is. This in turn means that, instead of subconsciously outsourcing difficult feelings to the voices, I am accepting and coping directly with my emotional life. On a couple of occasions, the voices have given me knowledge concerning what I've been experiencing. When listening, with open minded compassion, I can occasionally benefit by gaining more understanding about the voices.

Valerie Levey [11]

Chapter 2

What is Compassion Focused Therapy? And how can it help support voice-hearers?

Chapter summary

So, what is Compassion Focused Therapy (CFT)?

In this chapter, we will be explaining the main ideas behind the CFT approach. We'll start by touching on the scientific background to CFT, particularly the science of how evolution has shaped our brains into patterns for things like social roles and relationships. Although this information is important for explaining why CFT can be effective, we also don't want anything too technical to get in the way of what we think is most useful for you and your self-help journey, so we'll keep this section quite brief. However, for those who are interested, we will signpost you to where you can read more on the science of CFT applied to voice-hearing.

We will then explore this word *compassion* in detail by asking:

- What is compassion?
- Why do we need compassion?

As you'll see, one reason why we need compassion is that our brains are naturally very tricky and cause all sorts of problems for us. For example, our brains have a natural preference for paying attention to threats and are far more concerned with our protection than our happiness. We will describe how CFT aims to shift our mind's patterns away from *threat*-focused (giving and receiving threat) towards *compassion*-focused (giving and receiving care).

What is Compassion Focused Therapy (CFT)?

An approach to mental health informed by human evolution

CFT is an approach to mental health and well-being that tries to understand how and why our brains work the way they do. CFT is an evolution-informed approach, which means that it is particularly interested in how human brains and minds have evolved over time to perform certain jobs for us, such as protecting us

DOI: 10.4324/9781003166269-3

from danger and avoiding harm. The basic idea is that there are built-in patterns in our brains that work in the same way that codes work in a computer; essentially a series of "*if* A happens, *then* do B" instructions that have become hard-wired into us over many millions of years. Let's take the earlier example of avoiding harm. In such a situation, the process in the brain would be something like this:

> *if* there is danger, *then* increase heart rate and muscle activity to run away.

However, what if we were in a situation where the "run away" response wouldn't work and escape was impossible? In that case, a second process might be needed, such as:

> *if* there is inescapable danger, *then* demobilise, shut down, and go into a "defeat" state.

If we are struggling with our mental health, the CFT approach would be to try and understand which patterns (and processes) are being activated and why. Is my mind in a threat-protection mode right now? If so, what are the threats that I'm protecting myself from? Or, if my mind seems to be frequently in a threat-protection mode, even when there are no obvious threats around in the present, which past experiences am I remembering that's causing me to feel afraid and causing my threat system to remain on high alert?

Mental health difficulties of all kinds (from depression and anxiety to psychosis-related experiences such as distressing voices and unusual beliefs) are approached by CFT in the same way. In other words, CFT tries to understand the purpose of these experiences and emotional states using the framework of human evolution. Therefore, instead of asking the question "What has gone wrong in my brain?", CFT is more interested in asking questions like "Why is my brain responding to this situation in this way? Which evolved systems are being activated? What is the purpose of activating these systems?" (We will specifically explore possible functions of voice-hearing in Chapter 6.)

How social systems affect our relationships

Humans are a very social species. In fact, relationships are vital to us, and one of the reasons that humans have been so successful over time is because of the way we are able to work together to promote the well-being of the group (interestingly, some of the most intelligent species in the animal kingdom are also highly social, such as elephants, primates, and dolphins). As such, there are a number of patterns in our brains that have evolved over time to work on *social* functions. These are called "social mentalities" [12], which is quite a technical term but basically just means a state of mind which helps to create social roles for us and organise our relationships. For example, some create roles that organise *cooperative* relationships, such as when we are in the role of a "caregiver" (looking after someone else) or "care receiver" (being looked after ourselves). Others organise more *competitive* relationships, such as when we are in situations like "winner-loser" or "powerful-vulnerable". As we mentioned in Chapter 1, the two key mentalities of interest in this book are the *"threat-giving – threat-receiving"* mindset (which researchers often call our *"dominant-subordinate"* mentality) and the *"care-giving – care-receiving"* mindset.

Importantly, the same social mentalities that organise our relationships with others also organise the relationships we have with ourselves. So, depending on which social mentality is switched on, I can either be in a competitive relationship with myself (such as when I am being self-critical), or I can be in a caring relationship with myself (such as when I am being self-compassionate). There is research evidence showing that our self-to-self relationship can often mirror the self-to-other relationships we have experienced in our lives [13]. So, for example, if we have experienced a lot of criticism and hostility from powerful people in our life, the "threat-giving – threat-receiving" social mentality will have been well activated and trained, and may then become a main template for how we relate to ourselves. It's as though the power relationship has now become *internalised*, with one part of us doing the criticising and attacking, and another part of us receiving the criticism and defending. From a CFT perspective, this is one of the major factors leading to mental health difficulties, and one of main processes CFT seeks to help people with. For example, the CFT approach aims to help us learn how to:

a)   notice when we are in a *"threat-giving – threat-receiving"* mindset, and
b)   shift into a *"care-giving – care-receiving"* mindset

Interestingly, social mentalities can also be important in shaping the kinds of relationships we have our voices. So, for instance, when a dominant-subordinate mentality is switched on, a voice might be in the dominant role (e.g. criticising, shaming, and threat-giving), and as the voice-hearer, we might be in the role of being under threat and having to defend ourselves (threat-receiving). In 2019, we published an open-access review paper with some colleagues that was written for a scientific audience, and therefore, it goes much deeper in the scientific theory and research evidence for evolved social mentalities in voice-hearing [14].

Later in the book, we will have a chance to walk through these steps more slowly together with exercises to try out (Chapters 4 and 5), as they are very important for how we can begin to apply CFT in our lives. The plan is that the more we can practice organising our minds and relationships using caring and compassionate motives (rather than threat-based and competitive motives), the more this will build up experiences of social safeness and connection and will support several physical processes in our bodies that are important for our well-being. This book will help us to try out some ways of developing a compassionate mind, and of bringing compassion into our relationships with others, with ourselves, as well as with our relationships with voices.

What is compassion?

What does the word compassion mean to you?

To start with, it might be helpful to spend a few minutes thinking about what this word "compassion" actually means to you. We often ask this question at the beginning of our CFT workshops and training, and it's always interesting what a mixture of responses we hear back. A lot of the associations people come up with have a warm and positive tone, with words like "kindness", "empathy", and "love". However, many other associations we hear can suggest quite a different tone, such as "soft", "fluffy", and "weak". We think this is really important, because it recognises that people often have very different ideas and feelings around this word *compassion*. For some people, it can signal feelings of safeness, comfort, and trust. For others, it creates an image of vulnerability and naivety, perhaps even something that should be feared or avoided.

So, when *you* think about the word compassion, what feelings come up for you? Do you have any concerns or worries about it? If you do, remember that's understandable, and absolutely fine and normal. In our experience, having positive, negative, or mixed feelings about the word compassion is very common, and shared with many other people. If it feels okay, perhaps take a minute to see if you can notice what your feelings are about this word.

CHECK-IN BOX

How are you doing? We just wanted to check in with you about how that feels – being invited to notice your feelings about something?

We know from experience that many people try not to allow themselves to notice their feelings. This is totally understandable for all sorts of reasons, including that some emotions might feel unpleasant in the body.

Common feelings include sadness, fear, anger, joy, and disgust. These are all experienced slightly differently in the body. There is a good chance that you will be more comfortable with some of these feelings than others. That's okay. That's exactly what it's like for us too.

If this is difficult, it's fine to take a break and move your attention away to focus on something else, such as the way the book feels in your hands or by looking at something in your environment. Then later, when things are settled, you might feel more comfortable to come back to feelings again. Remember to take care of yourself. And, if you can, try not to judge yourself harshly for having these feelings. Whatever they are, they are a normal response and are happening for an understandable reason.

Now we'd like to consider a quick example to discover what else you might know about compassion. Imagine that someone you care about phones you up one day sounding very upset because they have just had an argument with their boss.

- How would you listen to them?
- How would you feel towards them?
- What would you say?
- What would your voice tone be like?
- What would you like to do to help them?

You can also think of a similar example the other way round, where you imagine that you are the person who's upset, and how you would like people to feel about you, or behave towards you, in that moment? How would you like them to support you? Being able to imagine these things shows that you already have a natural knowledge about compassion. Compassion is really about being sensitive to the distress of either yourself or another person (instead of being, say, critical, judgemental, and dismissive), and it is also about trying to work out what you might say or do that could help with this distress.

So, although the word compassion itself can be complicated, and sometimes off-putting for people, we think it's important to recognise that not only do you already know a lot about compassion, but there are also many compassionate skills that you already have (possibly without even realising it). Compassion is not something external to you and out of your reach. It is something that you currently own, and this book is about helping you to find ways of tapping into this and bringing it more into your life and relationships.

The CFT definition of compassion

In CFT, there is a particular way of describing compassion that is typically used by Paul Gilbert, ourselves, and others involved with the development, sharing, and teaching of CFT ideas:

> *A sensitivity to the suffering of self and others with a commitment to try and relieve and prevent it.*

This definition can be divided into two main parts. Firstly, there's the sensitivity aspect, which involves *engagement* and connection with suffering, difficulty, or distress. Secondly, there's an aspect about a commitment to do something about it, which is more about taking *action* to reduce the suffering. Let's explore these two aspects in a little more detail:

1   *Engagement*: The first aspect of compassion involves the ability to understand, approach, and engage with difficulty or distress. Just think about that for a minute, what that actually means – to engage with something really difficult and distressing. Now that is hard! The easier option would be to turn away. So, turning towards suffering is hard, and it takes strength and courage. Does that sound "fluffy" or "soft" or "weak" to you? Absolutely not. In this definition, compassion is very much about strength and courage to move towards, tolerate, and engage with something difficult and painful (whether it's your own pain or distress, or someone else's).

2 *Action*: The second aspect of compassion involves the desire and motivation to do something about the distress; to uproot the causes, and to try and prevent this from causing more distress in the future. Again, let's just think about what that actually means. To do something helpful with distress is likely to require a certain confidence, knowledge, and skill: confidence that I *can* be useful; wisdom about *how* to be useful in the particular situation; and the skills, tools, or resources to actually carry this out. And even with all these qualities, it still might take some time, so this intention to be helpful is also likely to require patience, persistence, and dedication.

Now that we've explored the CFT definition of compassion, and broken it down a little, how does this definition fit with your initial feelings about the word? We think that having a good understanding of what we mean by compassion will really help when reading this book, so we have included a resource box about compassion which will make it easier for you to refer back as you go through the chapters.

RESOURCE BOX

SUMMARY: The two aspects of compassion

The two aspects of compassion

1. Being aware of the distress and difficulties experienced by ourselves and other people.
2. Doing something about the distress and difficulties by learning what is helpful and then taking steps to reduce or prevent it.

EXERCISE: Your instinctive knowledge of compassion

1. Imagine you were with somebody who was struggling with similar things that you've struggled with yourself in the past. Maybe this person is frightened, feeling lonely, or is hearing voices that are upsetting them. How would you like to show compassion to that person? What might you want for this person? (To feel better/to be heard/to be less lonely?) How would you like to talk to them and behave with them? How would you feel towards them?
    (think about this for minute, and if you like, write some notes down)

    . . . .

    . . . .

2. If you could be very compassionate towards someone you care about who is struggling, how do you think they would feel about it?
    (think about this for minute, and if you like, write some notes down)

    . . . .

    . . . .

    That's great. That's your instinctive knowledge of compassion right there.

Why do we need compassion?

The human brain is a wonderfully complex and ingenious thing. However, an important reason we need compassion is that our brains are also a total mess! Yes, they really are. They are very complicated and naturally disruptive, and they cause all sorts of problems for us. If you think about it, our human brain was not perfectly designed for our modern life today in the 21st century. Scientists suggest that our brains have evolved over many millions of years, through many different time periods, and in environments which were vastly different to those in which we live today. In this section, we will walk through some of the interesting, but potentially very problematic, quirks of our "*tricky brain*" – each of which has a big impact on our mental health and well-being:

1   Our brain has a natural threat bias.
2   Our brain creates loops.
3   Our brain gets shaped by our motives and emotions.

Don't worry if some of these terms are unfamiliar. We will explain each of them as we go along.

Our brain has a natural threat bias

In our evolutionary past, our ancestors' daily routines would be unrecognisable compared to the ones we have now. There were long periods where every time our ancestors left their homes (which were probably caves in those days), they would have been faced with dramatic life-or-death situations – for example, fierce predators sniffing around for a human lunch! These are the contexts in which human brains developed. In order to survive these environments, the brain had to develop a very powerful and effective threat-response system. Although this was essential for helping our ancestors to survive, and to pass their genes on to us, the strong threat-related instincts and emotions that we've inherited can cause all sorts of problems in our modern lives. For example, when a powerful, threat-based emotion such as anxiety switches on, it can suddenly take complete hold of us, dominating all our attention, our decisions, and our actions. The actual threat might seem minor compared to what our ancient ancestors had to deal with, yet the response in our bodies can still be nearly as overwhelming. This is something we'll talk about more in the next section, when we think about how these aspects of our "old brain" have adapted to a modern environment.

As we discussed earlier, it's important to remember that while our threat system can be very helpful, it doesn't function for our happiness. It doesn't care about our mental well-being, or whether we can experience "inner peace". Its only job is to be on constant alert for threats of harm and injury so that it can take rapid action to protect us. It works on the principle of *"better safe than sorry"*. So, when we say it is naturally biased towards threat, what we mean is that all its attention goes towards over-checking, over-estimating, and over-reacting to potential dangers. In the book *"Good reasons for bad feelings"* [15], Randolph Nesse compares this process to a smoke detector – in order to keep us safe from the danger of fire, we unfortunately have to put up with the occasional false alarm (for instance, when there's no fire but we've just burnt the toast!) The point is that it's better to be safe – and to over-detect danger with false alarms – than to be sorry.

We often think that things like our brains should work perfectly and, if they don't, that something has gone wrong, or there's something wrong with *us* and it's in some way our fault. But, as we'll see in this book, for much of the time it's really nothing to do with us at all. Instead, it's often very much to do with this *tricky brain* of ours. Our brain is not perfectly designed for our lives today – and that's not our fault. That's just the way it is. We're all in the same boat with this together. Our brain is structured in a way that makes us quite vulnerable to mental distress and suffering, and that's one of the key reasons why we need compassion, for each other and for ourselves.

CHECK-IN BOX

How are you finding this? Is this new to you, the idea that we all have tricky brains? It's not the sort of thing we learn about in school!

We're also aware that we've made a few references to the scientific theory of evolution, which may not be everyone's preferred way of understanding of how humans came to be. That's okay if it isn't. It might still be helpful to look together at how brains function, how they get influenced by different emotional processes (regardless of how that came about). There are many religious people, for instance, who hold the position that evolution itself was a process set in motion by God. These are interesting questions, but slightly outside the scope of this book!

Our brain creates loops

Let us now explore this *tricky brain* of ours in a little more detail. The more we can understand about how the brain works, and the more we recognise that it's really not our fault, the more this might help us open up to compassion and recognise the role of compassion in our lives.

If we take a (simplified) look at different brain functions, we can see that some of them are much older than others. The older brain functions, which in CFT we call the "*old brain*", are very similar across many different species. However, more recently evolved brain functions, called the "*new brain*", are more pronounced in humans. The *old brain* has more primitive responses and motivations (e.g. detecting and avoiding danger, and forming relationships), and the *new brain* is characterised by reasoning, imagination, and forward-planning. All these processes are helpful, but sometimes they may interact in unhelpful ways. For example, we may find ourselves worrying about a future threat, even though it's not that likely to happen, or we may associate things that are important to us, such as socialising, with danger.

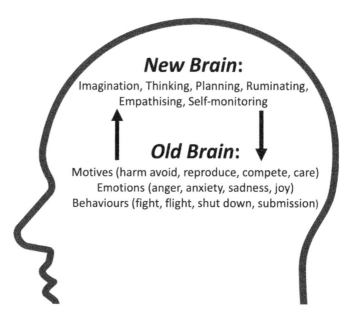

Interaction of old and new brain creates "loops"

It is not our fault that humans have these interactions between new brain and old brain. It is down to the design of our brain. The *new brain* fuels *old brain* emotions and responses, and the *old brain* fuels *new brain* anticipation, thoughts, and images. This basically means that one part of our brain fires up another, and so on, until the whole system gets caught in a vicious circle. In

CFT, these are called "*loops*" (please see the diagram. Also see the practical box for details of a freely available video that we, at Balanced Minds, helped to produce to describe this.) To give one example of this process, imagine how a zebra reacts after it has escaped from a lion. Before too long, its heart rate has returned to normal and it's peacefully grazing again like nothing happened. However, think of how a human would react in the same situation. Even though we had escaped, we might spend time tormenting ourselves with all the terrible things that *could* have happened and feeling anxious about them (what if I'd been badly bitten? What if I'd died? – Who would have taken care of my children? What if I'd needed time off work then lost my job?). We might never want to go to a safari park again. We could wake up in the middle of the night in a cold sweat remembering how scared we felt. Even though our *old brain* reacted the same way as the zebra's did to help us escape, our new brain has now come along to make everything much more complicated for us in coping with our experience.

We all have loops because this is just how our brains are designed. However, there will be many differences from one person to another about which loops are most active and present in our minds and lives. For example, some of us might have loops that are very focused on anxiety for social situations. In this case, our *old brain* is likely to be creating fear-based emotions and preparing our body to avoid or run away. Meanwhile, our *new brain* might be imagining ourselves looking "weird", and worrying about negative comments from other people ("What if they don't like me? What if I can't think of anything interesting to say?"). We might also start guessing or anticipating that something terrible will happen, or maybe we'll start remembering that time last year when something embarrassing did happen – and convincing ourselves it'll happen again. After listening to our new brain run through all these possible options, we might then decide to just avoid the potential threat entirely and not go to the party like we planned. The old and new brain have essentially started to fuel each other and wind each other up, which can then keep us stuck in a loop.

This is an example of a socially anxious loop, but there are many others that we are prone to being caught in: angry loops, depressive loops, self-critical loops, just to name a few. There might also be loops about feeling others are trying to harm us, or about getting overwhelmed and unable to cope. The list goes on, and the important point is that the design of our brain, while brilliant, also has a lot of problems with it. It makes it very easy to get into these loops and rather difficult to get out of them without some help. And in the long term, this can keep us feeling very unhappy. It's really not our fault that we've inherited this human brain of ours that does this. We're all in the same boat together with our tricky brains, and the first steps to compassion are being open to some of the difficulties and suffering that we are all up against as humans – followed by a desire to relieve or reduce suffering. We can become aware of what our minds are doing, and we can also try to understand it. This can then, in turn, help us to make choices to enable us to move forward.

PRACTICAL BOX

VIDEO: Developing a Compassionate Mind (First half)

You can find the "Developing a Compassionate Mind" video on YouTube and on the webpage: www.relatingtovoices.com/videos

The first half of this video describes how our old brain and new brain interact together to create "loops". We all have loops due to our brain design, and it might be helpful to now just spend a bit of time noticing what types of loops you often have going on in your mind.

EXERCISE: Your daily loops

1. What are your typical daily loops?
    (think about this for minute, and if you like, write some notes down)

    . . . .

    . . . .

2. Over the last week, can you think of times when you might have got stuck in loops?
    (think about this for minute, and if you like, write some notes down)

    . . . .

    . . . .

Thank you. Remember loops are built in, they're things we all share. It's not your fault.

Our brain gets shaped by our motives and emotions

The "daily loops" exercise shows us how, through no fault of our own, our minds can become organised and shaped in particular patterns. This is similar to what we were describing about *social mentalities* at the beginning of this chapter. However, an important difference is that social mentalities are hard-wired patterns that we are all born with (shaped by many years of human evolution) which are then activated in our daily life. Loops, on the other hand, are patterns that are shaped by our individual, day-to-day emotional experiences. It's a little bit like a computer. There's built-in hardware (the actual machine), then later on some software is installed

(Microsoft Word or Excel, for example) that uses the hardware to run. Hardware and software are the same across different computers, yet each person might set up their software to run a bit differently depending on how they use their computer.

CHECK-IN BOX

Don't worry if you're finding some of these descriptions of brains a bit confusing. If you are, it's not your fault! If anything, it's ours for not explaining it in a way that makes sense to you. You might find some of the internet resources listed in the Appendices help to make it clearer, and there are other CFT self-help books (not specifically about voice-hearing) that describe these processes as well. Also, remember, you can always put this more science-based section to one side and come back to it later. Whatever feels most helpful to you.

In general, it can be useful to think of our human brain as a "pattern generator". Our brain is constantly creating patterns, some of which are activated by changing environmental and emotional states (in the present moment), some of which are learned through repeated experiences (from past events), and some of which are inherited from many years of human evolution.

Exploring emotions with multiple selves

We will now turn our attention to the patterns that are created by our emotions, focusing specifically on what CFT founder, Paul Gilbert, calls "the big three": anger, anxiety, and sadness [16]. Because these different emotions have different purposes, they each create very different patterns in our minds and bodies. In other words, each emotion affects our attention, our thoughts, our bodily sensations, and our behaviour. In CFT, we think of these different patterns as being a collection of sub-selves or mini-selves. This invites us to think a little bit differently about ourselves, and how complex we actually are as humans. From film or television, or perhaps within mental health services, you might have heard of something called Dissociative Identity Disorder (DID), or the idea of "split" or "multiple personalities", so it's important to let you know that that's not what we're describing here. DID is a complex experience that can result from extreme trauma and stress in a person's life. However, CFT's idea of multiple selves is something which we believe is shared by all human beings, regardless of their life experiences.

So, what are these selves? Mostly (at least in Western cultures) we tend to think of ourselves as having one, whole, single sense of self – what we refer to as "I", "Me", or "Myself". Of course, this is true in a general sense, but another way of understanding it is that all of us are actually a collection of *multiple selves*. Right now you might be thinking "that's certainly not true for me – I know exactly who I am!", so please let us explain what we mean. As humans, all of us have different (sub) versions of ourselves; for example, there is our "angry self", our "anxious self", and our "sad self". All of these multiple selves have their own motives, ways of paying attention, thinking about things, bodily sensations, and ideas about how to respond. They even have their own memories. If you are interested, this practical box guides you through an exercise where you will be introduced to your own multiple selves, namely your angry, anxious, and sad self.

PRACTICAL BOX

VIDEO: Developing a Compassionate Mind (Second half)

You can find the "Developing a Compassionate Mind" video on YouTube and on the webpage: www.relatingtovoices.com/videos

The second half of this video describes how emotions from our old brain create loops which shape our minds in different ways. Because of this process, we can think of these as our different emotional selves: angry self, anxious self, and sad self.

EXERCISE: Your multiple selves

For this exercise, we are inviting you to think about an argument that happened recently in your life. We don't want this exercise to be upsetting though, so maybe choose an argument that's not still ongoing, or still raw in your mind, but rather one that's finished or resolved. Please spend a moment remembering what the argument was about, where you were, and who the argument was with. If you like, you can close your eyes to try and picture the scene of this argument in your mind.

Angry self: First of all, let's focus only on the part of you that is angry about this argument. Allow yourself to feel this angry part in your body now. When you feel connected to your angry part, or angry self, just go through these four steps:

1. *Thoughts/mind:* what's going through the mind of your angry part? What thoughts does this part have about this argument? Do any words or phrases come to mind?
2. *Feelings/body:* notice what that feels like and whereabouts you feel that angry part in your body.
3. *Behaviour/urge:* what does your angry self feel like doing? What's the urge? If it could, how would the angry self act?
4. *Preferred outcome:* what does your angry self want as the outcome? What would be a good result of this argument for your angry part?

Okay, so now just make a quick note of each of these aspects in the first column of the following table.

When you've captured that, we're just going to get grounded again by bringing your body a bit more upright and taking take a few slow breaths. Use your breath to just let the angry self settle, and to slowly allow this part of you to ease away. As the angry self leaves your body, perhaps you might want to say "thank you" to it for being there with you for a while and sharing that information with you.

Now, repeat all the same steps for the anxious self, and then again for the sad self. Remember to fill in the information in the table for each self, and remember to thank them for providing that information, and for being there with you today.

Angry self	Anxious self	Sad self
Thoughts/mind	Thoughts/mind	Thoughts/mind
•	•	•
•	•	•
Feelings/body	Feelings/body	Feelings/body
•	•	•
•	•	•
Behaviour/urge	Behaviour/urge	Behaviour/urge
•	•	•
•	•	•
Preferred outcome	Preferred outcome	Preferred outcome
•	•	•
•	•	•

Thank you – and thank you to your selves.

One of the difficulties created by this process is when our emotions (or our different selves) are in conflict with each other. Here are some common examples of the types of conflicts and complications that can exist in the *relationships* between our multiple selves:

* Our anxious self might be afraid of our angry self.
* Our angry self might be masking some deep sadness behind it.
* We might be stuck in sad self to avoid feeling underlying anger.
* Our anxious self might be highly active, and constantly switched on, to avoid feeling anger, sadness, or both.

In these examples, we can see how some problems might occur when we get very caught up with one particular self, because it can cause *too much* access to that emotion. On the other hand, different difficulties might occur when we find it very hard to access a particular self because we are having *too little* access to that emotion. Have a think about your own relationships with your multiple selves. Which of them – angry, anxious, or sad – do you find easiest to access? Which of the multiple selves – angry, anxious, or sad – do you find hardest to access? Remember, whether it's easy or difficult is not your fault. For example, some of us might have been punished for showing anger when we were growing up so have learned to reject our angry self. Or we might feel that if we allow ourselves to acknowledge our sad self then the resulting grief would be too much for us to cope with. Or perhaps, we feel that if we don't pay all our attention to our anxious self then something terrible might happen. We will talk more about some of these ideas later in the book, so don't worry about trying to analyse your different selves at this point unless you want to. At the moment, all we want to do is simply recognise that they're there and how we think and feel when they're in charge.

CHECK-IN BOX

How's it going? We're talking about noticing feelings again. How is that for you?

Many of us find it difficult to notice our feelings, particularly threat-based emotions like fear and anger. That's understandable. They're supposed to be quite strong experiences because, at the end of the day, they're designed for our protection. Please take it easy. Be gentle with yourself, and only go as far as it feels comfortable to go.

Some people find it helpful to imagine that they're intentionally making space for an emotion in their mind. So, in a way, they are allowing or welcoming it into their awareness. There is quite a well-known poem by Jalāl ad-Dīn Rumi called "The Guest House" which offers a helpful metaphor for learning to greet our emotions in this way. If you're interested, you can read it online and see how Rumi compares our emotional experiences to different visitors, some of whom may be difficult to deal with, yet all of them should be welcomed by us (the host of the guest house), because of what each one could have to teach us. The poem is over 700 years old and shows how much instinctive human wisdom there is in learning to respect and value the role our emotions have in our lives.

So, please remember that emotions are in all of us, and they're there for a reason. If you find some of yours to be frightening or difficult, it's not your fault.

How can compassion help you?

So, let's re-cap! We have been describing our brain as a pattern generator, where day-to-day patterns can get us caught up in the same responses ("loops"). These patterns are shaped by our emotions (our "multiple selves"), and we have inherited patterns that were passed down through evolution to help us organise our social roles and relationships ("social mentalities"). In CFT, compassion is seen as another type of social mentality, which is linked to social motives that humans have evolved for caring (whether for themselves or for each other). Compassion, therefore, is another way of organising and shaping our minds.

In CFT, the claim is that when we are suffering or experiencing distress (regardless of the cause), then if we can access caring motives, and switch into our *compassionate mind*, we will have a better chance of dealing with that suffering. With our compassionate mind online, we will be better placed to *engage* with the suffering and distress, and to then do something about it. Earlier in this chapter, we defined compassion in terms of two keys aspects: the *engagement* and connection with suffering/distress, and the commitment to take *action* by doing something towards reducing it. So, when we talk about compassion shaping our minds, what we mean is organising our mind with patterns of motives, emotions, thinking, behaviour, and bodily responses in a way that will best support compassionate engagement and action.

Remember, as we were saying earlier, compassion is hard! Moving towards distress and pain with the intention to help is not easy and requires various qualities, such as the strength to tolerate distress, the wisdom to know how to be helpful, and the commitment to hold and keep a caring intention. The good news is that compassion, and these key qualities of compassion, can be trained. In the same way that we train our bodies and muscles before a challenging physical task (like running a marathon), we can also train and prepare our minds for the challenging task of compassion. CFT researchers have identified 12 specific skills (or competencies) that can be trained to help develop our compassionate mind. Six are qualities that help compassionate *engagement:*

1   care for well-being
2   sensitivity
3   sympathy
4   tolerating distress
5   empathy
6   non-judgement

And six are areas of skill development that help compassionate *action:*

1   attention
2   reasoning
3   feeling
4   behaviour
5   imagery
6   physical senses

We will keep these skills in mind as we go through the book. However, the main focus for us when talking about developing compassion will be the key qualities we've already mentioned: **wisdom**, **strength**, and **commitment**. Building these key qualities is what will prepare us for the challenge of bringing compassion to ourselves, to other people, and to our voices.

Compassion applied with voice-hearing

Through our experiences and work with voices and voice-hearers, we have come to understand *distressing* voices as aspects of our threat-protection system. Remember, the threat system is built into all of us, and it does an important job to keep us safe by detecting and responding to threats in the environment. Research has shown that unfortunately many voice-hearers often report life experiences involving social threat, such as bullying, discrimination, abuse, or other situations where they experienced large amounts of fear and powerlessness [17]. When our threat system becomes activated through these kinds of experiences, it not only shapes our minds but can also influence our future relationships, with both other people and our voices, but also with ourselves. For instance, if we have been bullied, attacked, or abused, this will switch on our "dominant-subordinate" mindset, which means that we naturally become more focused on the power of others (and voices), and to what we see as the powerlessness of ourselves. Other aspects of this mindset might involve experiencing feelings of defeat, inferiority, rejection, shame, more sensitivity to comparing ourselves to other people, and more likelihood of using protective strategies linked with our nervous system, such as dissociation, submission, and low mood.

A big question for this book, therefore, is: if we are distressed by hearing voices, how might we go about trying to re-shape our minds away from threat patterns and towards patterns that are more helpful for our well-being? It is not our fault that we find ourselves with these threat patterns switched on; these have been activated in our mind as a result of trauma, or previous experiences of being harmed or frightened by people who had more power than we did. This is our brain's natural way of trying to protect us from future harm, using the formula of "it's better safe than sorry" (remember, like the smoke detector that sounds an alarm *just in case*, even when we've only burnt the toast).

In this book, we will outline an approach that involves shifting our mindset from one that is based in threat (for example, patterns of feeling powerless and dominated) to one based in compassion (patterns of giving and receiving care). With a compassionate mind, we may be able to be more sensitive to our own distress, to act on that in a caring way, and to respond to the experience of being caring towards ourselves. Caregiving and care-receiving are associated with very different bodily states to that of dealing with threat. Instead, they create processes that help us feel safe. In attachment theory, which is the study of how humans form emotional bonds, such processes are called creating a *safe haven* and having a *secure base*. A safe haven helps us to calm down and manage our emotions in the face of high levels of distress. A secure base helps us to develop the courage to explore and engage with difficult parts of our experiences. If we were lucky enough to grow up in a safe community with parents who were very loving and supportive, then we will most likely already have an internal sense of a safe haven and a secure base. However, some of us grew up in environments where we felt very threatened and unsafe, which meant that we never really learnt these skills. Or perhaps our parents never learned them from *their* parents, and therefore didn't know how to teach them to us. Whatever the reason, CFT recognises that not everyone grows up with this particular "social mentality" switched on. However, the good news is that it has developed a set of techniques and practices that can help us learn these skills as adults, which we can then apply simply and peacefully within our everyday life.

This book will share some ideas and techniques for shifting into compassion and will guide you through the process of compassionate engagement with voices, as well the threat-based memories and emotions that may be behind voices. We may not recognise it right now, but there really is a compassionate mind built into all of us; and over the following chapters, we will be exploring various ways of accessing it, strengthening it, and then using it to start organising our relationships with ourselves, our emotions, and, of course, with our voices.

Part 2

Beginning the journey

Chapter 3

Safety and safeness

Chapter summary

What is safety and safeness – and what is the difference between them?

Although safety and safeness are often talked about as being the same thing, in this chapter, we will explain how this is actually not the case:

- Safety is focused on reducing threat.
- Safeness is focused on increasing comfort and security.

We will explore how safeness can be created *internally* (from our bodies) as well as *externally* (from our environment and relationships).

We will then guide you through some practices that can help you to start using your body to support your mind in feeling safer: *body posture, soothing breathing rhythm, facial expression and voice tone*, and *my calm place*. Finally, we will also guide you through developing your own "safety and safeness kit".

Introduction

One of the most striking features of our brains is how incredibly good they are at adapting and responding to our environments. In the same way that brains will adapt to threatening situations by using protective strategies (like dissociating, for example, and voice-hearing), our brains will also naturally adapt and respond to conditions of safeness, kindness, and nurturing. You only have to look at babies to see that our new-born brains are ready from day one to respond to caring, warm relationships and interactions. When babies are distressed and crying, the adults around them will instinctively start using things like closeness, facial expressions, voice tones, and touch to comfort the baby and reduce its distress – and the baby will respond to these, just as instinctively. That is how brains work.

As humans, we are wired up to be very sensitive to social signals of threat or safeness (in other words, whether a social situation makes us feel rejected and excluded or, alternatively, helps us feel accepted and connected). For example, one

DOI: 10.4324/9781003166269-5

consequence of a social interaction which makes us feel threatened is that it becomes hard to think clearly and to problem-solve. When our brains go into "threat-protection" mode, we may start fearing and blocking parts of our experience and emotions that are linked to vulnerability because we want to try and control these unpleasant feelings, or even avoid them entirely. However, when our social world makes us feel safe, our minds are more able to experience, process, and resolve these feelings. Social safeness can provide a *secure base* from which to confidently and compassionately engage with the more distressing parts of our experiences.

To give you a clearer idea of what we mean, imagine that you were about to go for a lengthy hike in the countryside and were preparing for it the night before. It's the longest walk you've ever done and you're feeling a bit nervous about it. Fortunately, the hotel you're staying in is warm and comfy, full of good food, and has a lot of friendly guests who've done the same hike themselves and have all sorts of helpful advice to offer. Now imagine that instead you were staying in a little draughty tent with a leak in the roof and no one to borrow supplies from when you realise some of yours have run out. Either way, you could still do the hike (that's another thing about our brains – they're very resilient!). But chances are, you'd feel more comfortable, confident, and prepared after spending the night in the hotel. It's a safe base from which to launch into something difficult; and it's the exact kind of feeling we want to help you to develop so you can have it with you whenever you need it.

Safety and safeness are different

Before we start this discussion, one thing that's important to know is that "safety" and "safeness" are not actually the same thing. Safety is when there is an absence of danger, but it is still different to *feeling* safe. With safety, our attention is focused on where the threat might be, so we are always checking around for it. Therefore, even though we are "safe" from threat (because it's not there right now), our stress levels can still be quite high. A bomb shelter, for example, is possibly one of the safest places there is, yet it is unlikely that anyone sitting in one would be able to unwind and have a good time, despite being physically unharmed. Safeness, on the other hand, is the presence of supportive factors that actively help to calm the threat system down. Safeness is when we are in the presence of people who we trust to take care of us, where we can feel more relaxed, and where we can turn our attention to being playful, curious, and explorative. Instead of a bomb shelter, safeness might be sitting on a beach where there's no one around but you and someone you trust and care about. Not only are you not thinking about the threat, but you are also actively focused on calming down and enjoying the company and scenery.

So, while safety and safeness are often clumped together, they are actually very different [16]. In terms of the three emotion systems (Chapter 1), safety is more linked to the threat system, and safeness is more linked to the soothing system. The presence of safeness has restful qualities that can reduce how active the threat system is being. And, in doing so, it can also activate other systems (like drive) that can support building close, caring relationships. Both safety and safeness are important when creating the right conditions to relate to our voices. In fact, later in this chapter, we will be developing a personalised "safety and safeness kit" for your own use. The safety elements of your kit will be focused on reducing the presence of threat signals, whereas the safeness elements will focus on increasing the presence of safeness signals (please see the following diagram). However, before we get on to your personalised plans, we would like to take you through some tips and resources for establishing safety and safeness that we have come across over the years, and that we have used for ourselves and with other people struggling with voices.

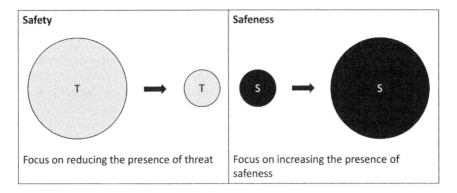

Safety	Safeness
Focus on reducing the presence of threat	Focus on increasing the presence of safeness

Safety and safeness

Safeness supports compassionate engagement, not avoidance

In this book, and in the CFT approach more generally, we are aiming to guide you towards building an internal sense of safeness, secure base, and safe haven. The central idea is that if we can create these conditions in our bodies and our minds, then this will give us a better chance of compassionately engaging with, and relating to, our voices. As we have been saying, distressing voice-hearing is rooted in the threat system, and so the focus of the current chapter is all about creating the right emotional resources to engage with that threat. It is important to recognise that while the soothing system often plays a role, we can engage with threat without necessarily having a calm mind. For example, a firefighter entering a burning building might be feeling very anxious (in their threat mind), but they also need to be grounded and focused with a compassionate intention to rescue people [18]. It's the same for when we engage with traumatic memories or emotions, or indeed with distressing voices. We need to develop the strength and wisdom to not necessarily have a calm mind, but a focused, grounded mind that will help us to tolerate and stay with distressing, painful experiences.

So, before we go any further, let's just be clear that we're not creating safety so that we can *avoid* all threat, and we're not creating safeness so that we can *soothe away* all threat. We are building safety and safeness so that we have a secure base from which we can *work with* the threat – to compassionately engage with the threat and do something to help. Our ability to compassionately engage might require some soothing or calming down of the threat system, especially if it is very active and over-powering. However, the intention is not to soothe it all away, in the same way that one might be able to do with some medications. Of course, it can feel very tempting to try to do this, because working with the threat system can be tough at times. How-ever, by doing this work, we are aiming to help address and uproot the *causes* of our struggles, rather than just the *symptoms*. This might feel harder in the short term, but in the long term, it will be much more helpful for us and our well-being. So, while you might well feel "soothed" by some of the practices and exercises that we cover in this chapter, our intention is not for you to use this book as some kind of sedative (as helpfully pointed out by some Italian CFT colleagues of ours in their article, "*Compassion is not a benzo*" [19]). If we only ever sedate the threat, then we cannot learn about it and resolve it – again, it's the idea of long term gain, not just short term relief. Our intention is to help you put the safeness strategies of this chapter to work later on in the book to support your compassionate engagement and action.

Safeness can activate threat, at least to start with

Before we go into the safeness practices, an important thing to say is that to begin with you might not feel soothed at all. In fact, some of you might have a very different response. You might notice that as you start to activate your soothing system, your threat system switches on; for example, your "anxious self" might pop up, or you might notice an urge to resist, or avoid, or to stop the exercise altogether. These are entirely understandable and common reactions for people, especially when trying out these exercises for the first time. If this happens, you might feel that you have done something wrong, but **you haven't**. You might think that there's something wrong with your brain, but **there's not**.

Remember that our threat system (which always obeys the rule: "better safe than sorry") will switch on when there is a chance, even if it's a very tiny chance, of a danger. So, if we notice that our threat system switches on when we do a "soothing breathing rhythm" practice or a "calm place imagery" practice, then that's because our threat system has learnt at some point in our life that feel-ings of soothing and calm are somehow risky. It's understandable why this might be, because when we are feeling soothed and calm, we are not monitoring for threats – we are "off guard". It may be that our threat system doesn't like that; instead, it prefers it when we are "on guard", especially if we have been hurt in the past. It is therefore very understandable that our threat system might switch on the first time we do an exercise like this; maybe the first few times in fact. It really is a case of having to *train our body* over time to *learn* that feelings of calm and safeness are okay. This might take a bit of practice, a bit like learning how to ride a bike – our body needs some time to get used to the feelings and the motions, and to learn that this is a safe thing to do. Those of you who have ever learnt to ride a bike will probably remember that for your first few goes, your threat system was switched on with the dial turned up to 10 (or in terms of the three circles diagram, with a big threat circle). However, over time, and with more practice, this started calming down to 8, 5, and so on, with the threat circle getting smaller each time.

I (Charlie) would like to share with you my first experience of doing a "soothing breathing rhythm – facial expression" practice (breathing with a friendly expression or half smile). It was with a group of people in a basement room in London, and I remember that when the course facilitator asked us to close our eyes and breathe with a friendly face, my threat system immediately shot up. I was suddenly very self-conscious about what my face looked like and how it was being judged – my threat self-monitoring system was immediately feeling mocked and humiliated as it started predicting all the negative judgements from the other people in the room. I had images flashing through my mind of my own face with a fake and forced "toothy grin", and images of people laughing at me. My heart was beating rapidly, I was sweating, and I had a strong urge to leave the room immediately. I peeked my eyes open slightly to have a subtle glance, fully expecting to see all the other people staring and pointing at me while laughing. But guess what: they all had their eyes closed and were happily immersed in their own breathing exercise. It was all an imaginary prediction; a "worst-case scenario" created by my threat system. I remember being embarrassed about that at the time, and when the facilitator asked the group for feedback after this exercise, there was no way I was going to share my humiliating ordeal with this group of strangers! However, now that I look back on this, I can appreciate that this was my threat system doing its job – to try and keep me safe. In that moment, my threat system decided that this was a new and unfamiliar experience for me: I felt vulnerable with a group of people I didn't know, and I couldn't take the risk of the terrible harm and hurt I would feel if I had been publicly shamed in this way. My threat system showed me what the shame would look like (complete with "high res"/HD images, mocking laughter, the lot!) so that I would take immediate protective action (my heart rate increasing, pumping blood and oxygen, and preparing my body for escape).

CHECK-IN BOX

How are you doing? We've been talking about some of the things that can come up from the threat system when we start practicing *safeness*. How are you feeling about this? How are your voices feeling about this? If your threat system could speak, what would it be saying right now about this idea of safeness?

It is entirely normal to have threat responses when we try out new things like this. It's also understandable if your threat system or your voices are a bit concerned about how safeness sensations could leave you feeling "off guard" or vulnerable. That's exactly how it made me (Charlie) feel when I was invited to relax into soothing breathing in the example I gave.

Maybe you could try and create a bit of *safety* before you start practicing *safeness*? For example, I decided after my basement breathing experience that the next time I was going to try a soothing breathing exercise would be on my own, definitely not in a room full of strangers! So, for you, maybe choosing a time and place to practice that is familiar, where you can trust you'll be safe, and you won't be interrupted.

If the threat system does pop up, like it did for me, don't worry – just remember this happens to all of us, and take care of yourself. You might decide to have a break and come back to it later when your threat system has settled again. This applies to trying out the exercises in this chapter, and throughout the whole book. As we go along this journey together, we'll be finding out all sorts of things about our threat system. For example, I discovered from my basement experience that my threat system is very sensitive to being shamed and humiliated in public. It's not my fault, but I'm glad I know that about myself now, because knowing things about ourselves can help us take better care of ourselves.

Internal and external safeness

We are now going to start taking you through some of the safeness techniques and practices that are used in the CFT approach to voice-hearing. We are going to separate out the things that can help create safeness in our body (internal signs) from the things that can help create safeness in our environment and social experiences (external signs). For your convenience, in the resource box we have summarised all the things that we cover in this section, for both internal and external safeness. We will then go through each of them in turn with some scripts and exercises so that you can try these things out for yourself.

RESOURCE BOX

SUMMARY: Internal and external safeness

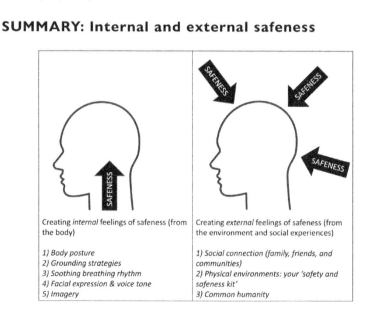

Creating *internal* feelings of safeness (from the body)	Creating *external* feelings of safeness (from the environment and social experiences)
1) Body posture 2) Grounding strategies 3) Soothing breathing rhythm 4) Facial expression & voice tone 5) Imagery	1) Social connection (family, friends, and communities) 2) Physical environments: your 'safety and safeness kit' 3) Common humanity

Both of these things (internal and external) are important in helping to create experiences of safeness. Some of them might also feel more in your control than others. For example, it might feel easier to start with focusing on creating grounding in your body than it is on creating compassionate communities and societies. The point here is that all of this is tied up together, and all these levels influence each other. There may be readers of this book who have more experience with political/social activism than others, and that's okay. Start by focusing on the bits that *you* feel comfortable with and build up from there. And remember what's been happening with the Hearing Voices Movement that we mentioned in Chapter 1? That is a substantial grass roots social movement, led by voice-hearers, which has had considerable impact in both communities and health services. It really shows that when people come together, we can fight for – and have influence on – the changes we'd like to see: the things we know will help to create a more compassionate world.

Internal safeness: preparing the body to help the mind

1) Body posture

To start with, let's spend some time focusing on how we can use body posture to support the experience of safeness. Whatever past relationship you might have had with your own body when it comes to creating feelings of safeness, it can still be one of your greatest allies for helping your mind. In this respect, our bodies are constantly sending signals up to our minds. Imagine that if your body was talking (with words) to your mind: it might be saying things like "I am sensing threat", or "I am feeling happiness", or "I am experiencing safeness", and so on. Depending on what kind of signal your body is sending, your mind will be picking this up, hearing this, and then shaping itself accordingly. So, if your body is saying "threat", your mind might start paying attention to where possible dangers might be, as well as potential escape routes. Your mind might also start bringing up a catalogue of memories about past threats, as these are things that could help you in keeping safe. Your body posture is a big part of this message. If your body posture is shaped in a way that says to your mind "I am in threat and I am protecting myself", your mind will switch into "threat mind", and will spiral into some of the threat-based loops that we described in Chapter 2. However, if your body posture is shaped in a way that says to your mind "I am okay and I've got this", then your mind will have a message that helps it to settle down.

Do you see what we mean when we say that your body can be one of the greatest allies for your mind? The body is a powerful messenger to your mind. And the great news about this is that body posture is something that you can control and have choices over. You can choose, for instance, which shape and position your body is in at any one time. It doesn't matter if you don't *feel* like the posture you have chosen, you can still arrange your body in that way. This is what actors do the whole time. On film sets, the director says "Right, act as though you're scared of this big CGI monster that you can't see", and then after a while says "Cut". In the time in between, the actors all switch on their "threat" posture for a bit, and then go for a coffee afterwards! We can all do this, too. We can all choose to switch into a different posture.

Why not have a try now?

- For 10 seconds, can you try and act as though you are about to be chased by a big shark (maybe imagine you are acting in the film, *Jaws*) . . .
- And now, for 10 more seconds, act as though your favourite sportsperson had just won a major tournament (maybe you're supporting in the crowd when the winning putt lands in the film, *Happy Gilmore*) . . .
- And finally, for 10 seconds, act as though you are now the most chilled out person in the world (if you've seen the film *The Big Lebowski*, you might take some inspiration from the character played by Jeff Bridges) . . .

Okay, so what did you notice? We just did some *pattern switching*, and this time, we used body posture to move around the different emotion systems. If you want to find out more about the power of body postures, there is an American researcher called Amy Cuddy, who has done some wonderful work on helping people to use body postures to support their minds. If you are interested, she has given a TED talk [20], which would be a good place to start finding out a bit about her work.

Now it's time to try out an exercise. In the practical box, we are going to guide you through a practice of using body posture to create safeness.

PRACTICAL BOX

EXERCISE: Body posture*

Sit in an upright and comfortable position on your chair and place both feet flat on the floor, about a shoulder-width apart. . .

If you like, you can now close your eyes, and just drop your awareness into your body. Just notice how it feels being seated here, how it feels with your feet flat on the floor . . . grounded . . . rooted . . . and stable. . .

If you need to shift anything in your posture slightly, just to help you get more grounded, let's just do that now . . . Maybe shift your hips a little to bring them into more of a balance . . . Maybe lengthen your spine a little to bring your posture a bit more upright . . . Maybe bring your shoulders back a little, to create more of an expansive, open feeling around your chest . . . Just creating a bit more volume and space in your lungs to breathe. . .

And just noticing that overall feeling of groundedness and stability in your body. . . .

Staying with that for a minute . . . noticing how that feels. . .

And as you notice this, you might just imagine that your grounded body is now sending a message up to your mind . . . it's saying "*I've got this . . .*"

Okay, so when you're ready, we can just finish up this exercise . . . and in your own time, open your eyes.

———

You can hear the audio recording of this exercise on: www.relatingto voices.com/audios

If you need a bit of time to think about how that made you feel, please take that time, and join us back here whenever you're ready.

2) Grounding strategies

Earlier we gave the example of a firefighter entering a burning building, and how this is not about being calmed or soothed, but instead being (1) grounded in the face of a threat, and then (2) focused in on it with a compassionate intent to help. We also said that this same process is important for compassionately engaging with painful memories, trauma, and distressing voices. We'll now share some thoughts about strategies to get grounded when the threat system is switched on (the threat circle is big). Being able to get grounded in these moments can help us to tolerate and stay with the threat instead of being overwhelmed by it. Grounding strategies can give us the strength to reconnect with our secure base, which is the platform from which wise and courageous compassion can occur.

In many grounding exercises, we can use our senses to guide us back to the "here and now". This can be particularly helpful if our threat system has triggered a painful memory which has caused us to dissociate or experience a flashback. Although this is another example of our threat system trying to protect us (from the traumatic memory), we may still want to get grounded and orientated again in the present moment so that we can carry on with what we were doing before the dissociation was triggered. One commonly used example of how we can use our senses do to this is by asking ourselves these questions:

- What are five things I can see around me?
- What are five things I can hear?
- What are five things I can touch?

Then, we can repeat the same questions, but with one less each time: four things we can see, hear, touch, followed by three things, then two, then one. All the while we are doing this, we can be taking slow, soothing breaths: in through the nose, pausing, then out through the mouth. If you need help working out the best way to time your breaths to reduce panic, then there are a lot of free resources available online (for example, balancedminds.com) that could be useful for you. We'll also talk a bit more about breathing rhythms in the following section.

Although our sense of smell didn't feature in that example, this can be a particularly effective route to getting grounded. Many voice-hearers and trauma survivors that we know carry items around in their pockets and bags that contain smells (for example, little bottles of scents) that have a grounding effect for them. A very powerful smell option for grounding us back into the "here and now" is a bottle of smelling salts. Of course, it depends what kind of effect you are looking for – smelling salts have a very strong smell, so might be effective at bringing you back into the room, orientated to time and place, but would not be so effective if your goal was to experience feelings of calmness and safeness (maybe a lavender smell or similar?). We will return to think some more about how we can use multi-sensory resources in the section on your "safety and safeness kit" later in this chapter.

3) Soothing breathing rhythm

"Soothing breathing rhythm" is a practice of slowing down the rhythm of breathing while also paying close attention to sensations of slowing and grounding in the body. The practice of breathing in this way can bring feelings of calmness, which can be helpful for steadying and grounding us when dealing with threat-based emotions and experiences. If you are interested in the biology of what's going on, the idea is that soothing breathing rhythm helps to switch on our parasympathetic nervous system (the PNS for short), which can have the helpful effect of balancing out our sympathetic nervous system (which underpins part of the threat system, often referred to as the SNS). For something so simple, it's really quite amazing, and shows how with practice we can use our bodies to help train our minds into feeling calmer.

For some people, breathing practices can be tricky at first. For example, bringing our focus into the breath or the body can itself switch on our threat system. As we mentioned earlier, it might be the soothing/calming experiences that are a threat to us (that sense of feeling "off guard", when our threat system has learnt that it's safer to stay "on guard"). If this is the case, remember that you are not the only one. This is common, and for most of us, it is best to take small steps in managing what we can do. Don't overwhelm yourself if breathing feels too difficult; just take a break and come back to it later instead.

There are several tools we have found helpful for voice-hearers when starting out with breathing practices. For example, if we are someone who struggles with paying attention to our breath, we can use visual aids and "apps" to help us focus. There are numerous apps that are available on smart phones. The one that we have on our own phones is called BreathingZone, but it doesn't matter which one you use. What the apps do is create a visual shape on the screen that moves in and out depending on the speed you selected in the settings. You can then breathe in and breathe out in time to the movement of the shape. The good thing about this is that you are very much in control of the speed, and you can choose a breathing rhythm that is comfortable for you. You can also choose other settings like sounds and colours that can make the breathing practices more personal. In the practical box, there is a soothing breathing practice that you can try for yourself.

PRACTICAL BOX

EXERCISE: Soothing breathing rhythm*

Sit in a comfortable, upright position, with your feet flat on the floor. Just notice that feeling of groundedness and stability . . . here in this chair, here in this moment. . .

If it feels okay, try closing your eyes . . . or, if you'd rather keep your eyes open, just settle your gaze in front of you. . .

In your own time, begin to settle your attention on the flow of your breathing, in . . . and out. . .

As you breathe, try to allow the air to come deeper into your body . . . down into your diaphragm, just below your ribcage . . . and feel that area move as you breathe in and out.

Now we'll begin to notice what different breathing rhythms feel like in the body, so play around with this for a minute . . . just notice what it feels like to breathe a little faster or a little slower than usual. And when you're ready, begin settling into the breathing rhythm that feels in tune with your body's natural soothing system . . . slowing down into a rhythm that feels comfortable, calming and soothing for you. . .

Just keeping that going for a little while . . . those smooth, even breaths, noticing how that feels in your body. . .

If at any time your mind wanders off or you get distracted, that's okay. That's what minds do . . . and when that happens, you can just gently bring your attention back to the breath and that feeling of groundedness in your body. . .

When you're ready, you can finish this practice by opening your eyes and coming back into being present here in the room. . .

---

*You can hear the audio recording of this exercise on: www.relatingto voices.com/audios

If you need a bit of time to think about how that made you feel, please take that time, and join us back here whenever you're ready.

---

4) Facial expression and voice tone

Interesting! My threat system switched on just by writing that heading! (Charlie writing). I think that my threat system must still remember that experience in the basement that I wrote about earlier. That was over 20 years ago; I wonder how long that experience will be engrained in my threat system? I still get the "toothy grin" image flashing through my mind, and a pang of fear in my body. But I am pleased to say that this doesn't distress me so much anymore. When I notice that image popping up, I try to bring a wise, knowing "nod" to it, understanding that it's just my threat system *doing its job*. It's just my evolved tricky brain doing its thing. It's not my fault. I have a slightly more light-hearted and playful relationship with it now. I am even grateful for it being there, because it has given me a story to write about in this book! So, I just wanted to say, while you're here, "thank you, threat system, you have given me a story that I can tell, which might hopefully help others with their own tricky brains".

Okay, so now that's out of the way, let's move on to focus on what facial expression and voice tone might be able to offer. There have been some interesting studies that have looked at how facial expression and voice tone can affect our body's calming responses to stress. In one facial expression study [21], the researchers asked participants to put chopsticks in their mouths, dividing them into groups depending on which way they were told to hold the chopsticks. The chopstick positions manipulated their facial expression, which meant one group was smiling, and the other had neutral expressions. While they held this facial expression, they were given a stressful task. The researchers found that smiling participants had lower heart rates during stress recovery when compared to the neutral group and concluded that facial expressions can have a positive influence in how our bodies deal with stress. Another group of researchers did a voice tone study [22], where they compared what it was like for young girls communicating with their mothers after a stressful task, either over text message or over the phone. They found that the girls who received messages showed higher cortisol levels (an indicator of stress) than the girls who communicated over the phone, with the additional element of voice tone. So again, this is evidence that voice tones can influence how our bodies deal with stress. With this in mind, let's try another practice.

PRACTICAL BOX

EXERCISE: Facial expression and voice tone*

To start off, just begin with engaging once more with your grounded body posture and your soothing breathing rhythm. . .

Once you've spent a little time re-connecting with that smooth, even flow of the breath, we'll introduce a facial expression. For three breaths, we will make a gentle smile and a kind facial expression, trying to create a feeling of friendliness in our face as if we want to show this to somebody we really like. And then we'll switch back to a neutral facial expression for three breaths, and then repeat. Here we go then:

- Three breaths friendly face
- Three breaths neutral face

- Three breaths friendly face
- Three breaths neutral face

Just notice any changes in feelings as you swap facial expressions. Okay, now we're going to use voice tones as well, once again changing between friendly and neutral. On the out breath, we are going to say hello to ourselves: you can practice saying "hello [your name]" in a friendly voice tone for three breaths and then in a neutral voice tone for three breaths. Here we go:

- Three breaths friendly face and voice tone
- Three breaths neutral face and voice tone
- Three breaths friendly face and voice tone

Again, just notice how this feels in the body as you switch from a friendly to a neutral voice tone . . . Maybe just think about that for a minute . . . about how that exercise went, and anything you noticed. . .

Okay, so before we finish, just check back in with your breathing rhythm and your grounded posture, here in the moment, and when you're ready, open your eyes.

———

You can hear the audio recording of this exercise on: www.relatingto voices.com/audios

If you need a bit of time to think about how that made you feel, please take that time, and join us back here whenever you're ready.

5) *Imagery*

Imagery is another very powerful way to create physical processes in our bodies, which means it's another tool we can use to create feelings of safeness, calmness, and contentment. If you think about it, our body does not really distinguish between whether a signal has been created externally (from the outside) or internally (from our mind). Either way, our body will still have a similar reaction. For example, if you have your favourite meal in front of you, your body will respond to that, maybe by creating saliva in your mouth or creating a rumble in your stomach. However, even when you just imagine your favourite meal, your body will still create a similar response. So, the body is reacting to both the meal (external cue) and your imagery of the meal (internal cue) in the same way. This means that imagery is a powerful tool that we can use to our advantage. If it works for meals, it can work for safeness! We're now going to practice this with an exercise where you will develop an image of your own *calm place*. If you like, you can prepare for this exercise by thinking about what you might like your calm place to be. Is it a place that you have been before, a place that is made up, or perhaps something inspired from a book or a film? How would you describe it? What can you see? What can you hear? What can you smell? What feeling does this create in your body?

When doing imagery exercises, some people can create quite clear and vivid images in their mind, while for many of us, the images are much more vague, fuzzy, and fleeting. Don't let this put you off, this is very normal. We're not expecting HDTV! If the images are unclear, maybe only snippets, or nothing at all, you can still just try and tune in to the feelings and tone being generated in the exercise.

PRACTICAL BOX

EXERCISE: My calm place*

To start off, begin by engaging again with your grounded body posture and your soothing breathing rhythm. . . . Just allow your breath and body to slow down a little. . .

When you're ready, you can bring to mind an image of a place that you think is calming. A place that gives you feelings of contentment and of peacefulness.

It's okay if there are just bits of image, or it's not very clear, or if no image comes into your mind straight away – if this happens, you can just notice the feelings instead, check back in with your soothing breathing, and then return to see what image might come into your mind.

When you have an image of some kind, spend a few moments paying attention to what you can see. Take a look around this place . . . noticing any colours, shapes, objects . . . Notice what you can see close by to you, and what you can see in the distance. . .

Now notice what you can hear . . . are there are any sounds that are present in this place? . . . . Just notice these, and what that feels like being here with these sounds. . .

Now notice whether there are any smells – any calming smells that are present here in your image. Just notice these . . . and notice how these smells make you feel. . .

Now notice any physical sensations . . . things that you can feel or touch, such as the warmth of the sun on your skin, or the feel of grass or sand which may be there around you. . .

Now just try to notice your relationship to this calm place. Just as you are feeling content and happy to be in this place, this place is also happy that you are there. The place is pleased that you have chosen it to be your calm place. . . . It welcomes you there and is happy to be able to help you feel calm and peaceful.

Just notice how that feels for a minute. . . . Knowing that this place wants you to feel supported, safe, and calm. . .

And when you are ready, just let the imagery fade away and open your eyes.

———

You can hear the audio recording of this exercise on: www.relatingto voices.com/audios

If you need a bit of time to think about how this exercise made you feel, please take that time, and join us back here whenever you're ready.

External safeness: creating the contexts in which we can experience safeness

1) Social connectedness (family, friends, and communities)

In this section, we will be focusing on our social environments, with an emphasis on exploring the role of relationships and connection in creating a sense of safeness. A lot of our understanding about the role relationships have in our emotional well-being comes from observing what happens in the interactions between small children and their caregivers (usually their parents) in the first years of life. John Bowlby, who developed "Attachment Theory" [23], studied many of these interactions and noticed that all humans are born with an evolved instinct to seek out closeness with a caregiver and to feel safe when that figure is close. What Bowlby was effectively saying is that our brains are "wired up" to feel comforted in the presence of loving, caring, and kindness. In CFT language, what this means is that experiences of closeness, connection, and social safeness have a natural (built-in) calming effect on the threat system, via the soothing system getting switched on.

The terms "secure base" and "safe haven" that we referred to earlier come from Attachment Theory, and the CFT approach to voice-hearing is heavily influenced by this work. This is partly why we want to really emphasise the importance of our relationships and social experiences in the process of compassionate relating to voices. If voice-hearing is an aspect of the threat system, and if social attachments can naturally calm the threat system, it follows that our sense of social connection can help us move towards a more peaceful relationship with our voices. The other important insight from Bowlby's work is that the child's experience of closeness with a caregiver also acts as a secure base for them when growing up – providing a platform from which they can develop the confidence and courage to explore the world and take risks. Again, this maps onto some important processes for voice-hearers. If voice-hearing is experienced as something distressing and feared, and if social connection can provide a secure base for courage and exploring, then it follows that our relationships can help us to develop the confidence and courage to start exploring our own distressing experiences. Social connection may therefore have a double role in helping us relate to our voices: both as a threat-calmer (safe haven) and as a basis for courage and exploration (secure base). Both can help us with compassionate engagement and action when relating to our voices.

CHECK-IN BOX

How are you doing? How is this feeling for you and your voices when you read about social connections? Many of us have had negative experiences with other people, so it makes a lot of sense if you, your threat system, and your voices, might have become wary of social connection, and maybe of people more generally. You might have learnt that it is safer to avoid social groups and occasions. Or perhaps you find it difficult to make friends and connect with others. If so, remember that this is not your fault. Many people have the same experience as you; and, like you, these difficulties have occurred for very understandable reasons.

Because of this, it might be frightening or frustrating for you to hear us talking about social connection as a good, helpful thing when you have mostly experienced it as negative. We fully respect and understand the wisdom of your threat system on this. For many people, it is true that experiences of social attachment and connection may *not* activate safeness and the soothing system, but rather the threat system. This can be due to our past experiences, particularly if we had difficult "attachment" experiences with our parents or caregivers in childhood.

For those of us with painful past experiences, it may understandably be harder for us to access the soothing/safeness effects of caring social experiences. Remember, it's not our fault. We didn't choose our parents, or the other kids who went to our school, or the people who were around in our life when we were growing up.

We cannot change the past. But in this book, we hope to be able to help you develop a more compassionate relationship to yourself, which involves an understanding of how your past may have shaped your threat system and patterned your mind. We hope that this book also provides some ideas, tools, and practices that can help you to *re-shape* your threat system and *re-pattern* your mind. For example, to learn how to feel safer in social situations, and to better understand the role of compassion in your relationships with yourself, with other people, and with your voices.

We realise that some readers of this book may be thinking that it's all very well talking about the role of social relationships, but so much of this is out of our control. You might be thinking, "but what can I do about it? I can't change how other people relate to me". That's right, there is only so much we can do, and sometimes we can do very little to influence how other people relate to us and our voices. Unfortunately, voice-hearing is still very misunderstood in society, which means some of the people we encounter might relate to us and our voices with threat-related responses, such as fear and uncertainty. As we described in Chapter 1, a lot of these social responses can leave voice-hearers feeling misunderstood, scared, and ashamed. There is some great work currently happening in trying to educate the public around less stigmatising views of voice-hearing, such as the work of the Hearing Voices Movement, but there is still so much more to be done. In fact, this was one of the main motivators for us in getting our heads together to write this book.

In this respect, we would just like to share a few thoughts for friends, family, or other supporters of people who hear voices, as we imagine that some of you may be reading this book as well. It can be very upsetting to know a friend or loved one is hearing voices. It can often leave those closest to that person feeling worried and confused themselves, wondering "What has gone wrong?" "How could this have happened?" and "How can we fix this?" In their worry and uncertainty, family and friends might unintentionally create an atmosphere of tension and high emotional stress. Again, this is understandable. From what we've been learning about our threat system ("better safe than sorry"), this is what tends to happen when our threat systems are switched on. It's not your fault, and it's not the fault of the voice-hearer in your life, who you really just want the best for. However, from what we have been saying in this chapter, this is not an ideal social environment for helping a distressed person to access their soothing system (safe haven) or to create a grounded and secure base to start exploring and understanding their voices. So, although these common reactions from family and friends are understandable, the kinds of social interactions that would probably be more helpful are those which are calming, accepting, and understanding, which involve careful listening, and where the voice-hearer's emotions are taken seriously and respectfully. One of us (Charlie) was actually asked about what advice he'd give to loved ones in an interview series for the *Psychology Today* website [24]:

INTERVIEWER: *If you had a loved one in emotional or mental distress, what would you suggest that he or she do or try?*

CHARLIE: *I would try not to suggest at first, but just be there and listen. If she is very distressed, then her mind is likely to be organized in such a way that it will be difficult for her to process and utilize my suggestions. So instead, I'd get alongside her, listen, allow, hold, wait, until she feels safe enough to start generating her own wisdom, ideas, and plans.*

The same would apply for her social environment (friends, family, networks, etc.) – I'd help her to create an environment in which she feels safe. We know from attachment theory that a safe base, within affiliative connections, is the ideal kind of platform for us to start developing the confidence and courage to explore our experiences.

If she does want to extend her network into health services, then again, I would favour a service that can facilitate her experiences of safeness. In my opinion, the treatment approaches that are most explicitly geared for this are Open Dialogue (external social safeness) and CFT (internal social safeness).

> *However, any warm, caring mental health worker will have the potential to help her feel calm, safe, validated, and understood.*

Extract from Eric Maisel interview series (2016) [24]

The Open Dialogue approach that was mentioned in this extract is a social network approach to mental health treatment that has been successfully piloted in Finland [25] and is also being evaluated across multiple sites in the UK's National Health Services [26], as well as in other parts of the world. Open Dialogue aims to create a consistent social network around a person struggling with their mental health: for example, their family, friends, neighbours, and mental health workers. These people meet regularly and allow a space to develop for careful listening and tolerance of uncertainty so that a dialogue can emerge. For more information about this approach, see the website www.open-dialogue.net. It's wonderful that there is a growing recognition of the importance of social networks and processes in mental health treatments, and in our opinion, the Open Dialogue approach is highly compatible and complementary with CFT.

However, perhaps the bigger challenge is how we can also extend this message out into wider society. How can we create compassionate communities? How can we create networks where difficult experiences such as voice-hearing can be expressed, explored, and safely discussed, without fear of social judgement or other negative consequences? This challenge will no doubt involve working with the media and with politicians. The media and other public figures have such a key role to play, especially when things like voice-hearing experiences are often portrayed as bizarre, frightening, and even dangerous. These messages shape the attitudes of our communities, and often lead people to send signals of threat, uncertainty, and avoidance, rather than signals of social safeness. In the Appendices and on the relatingto-voices.com website, we have included some resources and links to things that have emerged from the CFT community and the Hearing Voices Movement, which we think (and hope) are contributing to the compassionate communities of the future. There is still so much work to be done. Our hope is that one day, we will realise that voice-hearing is a part of human life; instead of being feared and pushed away by society, it might instead be listened to for our learning, self-knowledge, and growth.

2) Physical environments: your "safety and safeness kit"

In this section, we are going to think about the different ways safety and safeness can be helped by our physical environment. This includes places we can be, objects we can hold, activities we can be engaged with, and so on. Remember: safety is focused on protection from threat, whereas safeness is focused on finding and activating soothing resources (and which can, in turn, help calm the threat system). So, to give an example of physical environments, a place of "safety" could be a bunker during a war, staying protected from the enemy planes dropping bombs, whereas a place of safeness could be in the place you created in the "my calm place" imagery exercise mentioned earlier. As we've been saying, sometimes we need to focus on creating safety first (removing the threat) before we can focus on creating safeness. This would be true, for example, if someone was in a domestically violent or abusive relationship, where the priority would be safety and removing the source of danger. Because everyone is different in terms of things that help create safety and safeness, the best way to do this is through an exercise where you will develop your own "safety and safeness kit". This will contain a list of places, people, activities, or physical objects that help create safety and safeness. This exercise is adapted from the CFT for Psychosis Manual [27], but there has also been inspiration drawn from similar work by CFT colleagues, Kate Lucre and Neil Clapton, who developed the idea of a "compassionate kitbag" [28], which is a creative resource to help people think about the physical and practical resources they might need to support their sense of safety, safeness, and compassion.

RESOURCE BOX

My safety and safeness kit

Objects/possessions

Safety	Safeness
. . . .	. . . .
. . . .	. . . .
(e.g. a card with numbers to call when things feel difficult)	(e.g. a playlist of calming music, a collection of soothing/inspiring quotes, photos of people who care for me)

Places

Safety	Safeness
. . . .	. . . .
. . . .	. . . .
(e.g. locked room, park bench, a friend's/relative's house, church, café)	(e.g. a specific chair in my room/ house, looking at a certain view)

Activities

Safety	Safeness
. . . .	. . . .
. . . .	. . . .
(e.g. grounding exercise, naming five things I can see/hear, smelling salts, getting out for a walk)	(e.g. BreathingZone app, grounded body posture, smelling lavender oil, telling myself something reassuring, calm place imagery, a warm bath)

People

Safety	Safeness
. . . .	. . . .
. . . .	. . . .
(e.g. the crisis team, the Police, a suicide prevention helpline)	(e.g. the hearing voices self-help group, my sister)

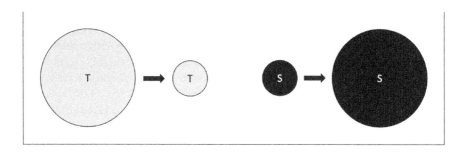

3) Common humanity

In Chapter 2, we described how the CFT approach is grounded in an evolutionary understanding of our human brains. Understanding our "tricky brains" in terms of how they have evolved over millions of years helps us to appreciate why there are so many things about them that can cause problems for us today in the 21st century. It's because our brains were not perfectly designed for modern life, as they have been developing and adapting over countless centuries to respond to a very different set of threats and challenges. Just to summarise, these were the main aspects we highlighted:

1   Our brain has a natural threat bias.
2   Our brain creates loops.
3   Our brain gets shaped by our motives and emotions.

Considering the evolutionary context is helpful for understanding why our brains are tricky (and understanding that it's not our fault), but it also does something else that is very important. It helps us understand that we are all in this *together*. We are all in the same boat. It's not a question of who has a tricky brain and who doesn't. We humans *all* have tricky brains. This understanding is sometimes referred to as a *common humanity* experience. There is no "them" and "us", there is "only us" (see Only Us campaign). And really appreciating that, and what that means, can itself help us to feel more connected. Life is hard. We all struggle. Experiencing problems with mental health can affect everyone at different times. It can come and go; some days are better than others. We don't have to identify ourselves as someone who is "mentally ill" or "mentally well", and we don't need to identify ourselves as someone with an "abnormal brain" or a "normal brain". Our human tendency to create divisions and categories are usually aspects of our "threat mind". And with our evolutionary understanding of common humanity, we can start trying to see the world, and our fellow humans, through the lens of our compassionate mind.

Chapter 4

Developing a Compassionate Self

Chapter summary

What is a Compassionate Self?

Essentially, a Compassionate Self is something we can learn to develop in order to relate to ourselves, to each other, and to our voices. It lives by the basic motto of being *helpful and not harmful*, and in this chapter, we will be helping you to start developing and training your own Compassionate Self. Firstly, we'll create a profile for it (including its intentions, characteristics, and qualities), then after that we'll begin to bring it to life through guided imagery and other exercises.

Finally, we'll develop a *Compassionate Mind Training Plan*, which will help you to practice and build these compassionate qualities and intentions over time. And of course, we'll also explore some of the common barriers and challenges you might face along the way – and how you can overcome them.

Introduction

Earlier in this book (Chapter 2), we suggested that we can think of our brain as a type of "pattern generator", and we introduced you to your multiple selves (angry self, anxious self, and sad self). These are the patterns and ways of thinking that are shaped by our emotions. The angry part of you thinks, feels, and behaves in a very different way to the anxious part; and the anxious part, in turn, thinks, feels, and behaves in a very different way to the sad part. This is why we refer to these parts as "selves" in CFT, because they pattern our brain in different ways. Remember too that these parts don't always see eye to eye on things! In any given situation, your angry self might want the complete opposite of what your anxious self wants. No wonder a lot of us struggle with our emotions – that's the tricky brain for you. Furthermore, while we've only talked about the angry, anxious, and sad selves so far, there are actually many more patterns in us. There is also a critical part (who we'll meet in Chapter 5), a joyful part, a proud part, a caring part, and so on. The thing about each of these multiple selves is

DOI: 10.4324/9781003166269-6

that they will each pattern our mind in different ways, affecting how we think, feel, and behave.

So, given we have brains that work in this way, why don't we think about which part (or self) would be one that we might *choose* to spend more time in. What kind of part would that be? And what if we could *choose* a part that could help support the other parts? What kind of part would that be? And what if we could intentionally create an ideal part that could help us with our struggles in life, and with our voices. What qualities would we want it to have? That is going to be the focus of this chapter, where we'll be discussing the idea of creating and training a part/self that can help us out with our tricky brains and our struggles in life. In CFT, we call this our "Compassionate Self". In the first half of this chapter, we will be focusing on developing your Compassionate Self, and in the second half, we will be focusing on some of the difficulties and barriers for developing compassion, and what we can do to help.

Your Compassionate Self

As a starting point, let's just remind ourselves about what we have already discovered about your instinctive knowledge of compassion. In an earlier resource box (Chapter 2, page 27), we asked you to imagine how you would want to act towards somebody who is struggling, and how you would want another person to behave with you if you were the one who was feeling overwhelmed. To help you bring this back into your mind, we now invite you to consider these three questions:

- Imagine that you were with somebody you care for who was suffering the same way you have. What sort of outcomes would you want for them? How would you feel towards them? How would you like to talk to them and be with them? How would you like to show compassion for them?
- Imagine that you had an ideal compassionate supporter who really cares about you. How would you like them to be with you? How would you like them to be with you when you are frightened, or maybe when your voices were feeling very difficult?
- If a compassionate friend treated you like this, how would that feel and how would that be helpful for you?

That's great, thank you for doing that. So, now we are ready to start creating your Compassionate Self. We will start off by thinking about some of the characteristics and qualities of this ideal helper – building up a "profile" of this ideal compassionate part of you. Once we've done this, we will bring it to life later in the chapter using imagery and acting techniques. In terms of qualities, there are some general ones that we suggest are shared by compassionate people (for example, being motivated to help rather than to harm). We will come to these general qualities in just a minute. But firstly, we want you to have a think about what specific qualities you would like *your* Compassionate Self to have in order to help you with the unique challenges/difficulties in *your* life. What are going to be the qualities that are most helpful for you and your voices? For example, if you would like your Compassionate Self to help you with very loud and threatening voices, you might think that it is important to have qualities like courage, level-headedness, a desire for well-being, and a non-judgemental attitude. If you experience a lot of anxiety in your life (in other words, if your anxious self is frequently online), then you might want your Compassionate Self to bring qualities of calmness, composure, and an ability to tolerate distress.

To start building up this profile, we'd like to invite you to write down a few thoughts about this in the practical box. If you're struggling to think of some qualities, it might be helpful to think of a real-life example where someone responded to your anger, anxiety, or sadness in a way that felt very helpful. Or you might like to think of a scene in a film or book, and the particular qualities that the character used to support someone in a positive way.

PRACTICAL BOX

EXERCISE: A profile of your Compassionate Self

What are the intentions and wishes of your Compassionate Self?
   (for example, does it want to be helpful, supportive? Does it want the best for people?)

. . . .

. . . .

   What are the physical characteristics of your Compassionate Self?
   (for example, what is its body posture, facial expression, or voice tone? Are any particular colours associated with it? Is it old/young, tall/short?

. . . .

. . . .

   Given its intention to be helpful, what are the qualities, skills, and strengths of your Compassionate Self?

. . . .

. . . .

What helps your Compassionate Self to be compassionate?

. . . .

. . . .

If your Compassionate Self had a motto, or tagline, that captures what it is all about, what would that be?

(for example, "I want to be a person who is helpful and not harmful" or something short like that)

. . . .

. . . .

CHECK-IN BOX

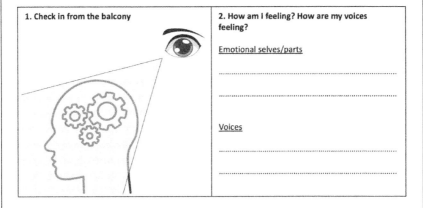

1. Check in from the balcony	2. How am I feeling? How are my voices feeling?
	Emotional selves/parts
	....
	....
	Voices
	....
	....

So how are you finding this? Any worries? What is coming up for you when you think about these compassionate qualities? Have you ever thought about some of these as being qualities that you might already have? Try not to worry if you haven't, because that will be the same for all of us. We are talking about ideals here, so there's a good chance that this might feel a bit distant from reality at the moment. Maybe your Compassionate Self character doesn't quite fit with your experience of other people in your life, or of how you are yourself. If so, that's fine! This is only the start of the process, so it's very normal to have doubts and questions. In fact, we (Charlie and Eleanor) had similar experiences the first time we started trying to imagine and think about our Compassionate Self.

At this point, another thing to consider is whether anything else is coming up when you focus on your Compassionate Self? Any thoughts or memories? Any emotions from your threat system? Any voices? If you haven't already, you can use the space next to the figure to write down any feelings, selves (angry, anxious, and sad), or voices that might be showing up. If you can, try not to make a judgement or emotional response about that. Just notice what it is, and what that part/voice is saying, as best you can.

We now would like to focus on three specific qualities of a Compassionate Self, which in CFT is sometimes called the "three pillars" of compassion. These are: 1) caring-commitment, 2) wisdom, and 3) strength. We want to spend a bit of time describing each of these to explain why we think they are such important *core* qualities of compassion:

Caring-commitment

Having the intention, desire, and motivation to care is central to compassion. This caring motive is the thing that helps shape our minds to become ready for compassionate engagement and action. Having a commitment to caring comes from our understanding that life is tough, and that people struggle with it – and that this is not our fault. And this motivates us to try and be helpful towards other people as well as ourselves.

Wisdom

Becoming motivated to be caring, helpful, and supportive in the world is wonderful, but it's not much good if we don't know *how* to be helpful. And this is where wisdom comes in. We need wisdom to guide compassion. We also need wisdom to truly understand the nature of suffering, both for other people and for ourselves. We need wisdom to understand common humanity (Chapter 3) – the fact that we all just find ourselves here on this planet, with these tricky brains of ours and a powerful threat system. This can help us to connect with the shared suffering that we all face.

Strength

Having the wisdom to understand that life involves pain and difficulty, and being committed to engage with it in a caring way, will inevitably bring us into contact with distress. And this is why strength is so crucial. Compassion brings us closer to life's struggles, and the qualities of courage, confidence, and strength will be important to help us engage with this. It is a way to not only manage the distress, but also to bring helpful actions to reduce or remove the causes of suffering.

It is now time to bring all these qualities to life – the three pillars, as well as the things you identified earlier in the practical box. To do this, we will guide you through two exercises where you have a go at stepping into the shoes of your

Compassionate Self and connecting with these qualities. The first will involve visual imagery, and the second will be about embodiment ("embodiment" in this context means trying to represent something, and we will do it using acting techniques). In these exercises, we are going to build on the work we have already done in Chapter 3. As we've been saying, safeness supports compassion. So, when we are preparing to engage our compassionate minds, and preparing to step into the shoes of our Compassionate Self, we always prepare the body first (posture, breathing rhythm, facial expression, and voice tone). In these exercises, we will also be using *mindfulness*, which is a strategy to notice where our attention is, and to refocus it onto the present moment. With mindfulness, we can learn to notice the distractions that occur in an exercise (for example, our mind "wandering off") and to gently – and kindly – bring our attention back to the focus of the exercise. If you are interested in practicing mindfulness as a stand-alone skill, there are many mindfulness audios freely available on the internet (for example, balancedminds.com).

PRACTICAL BOX

EXERCISE: Your Compassionate Self (imagery)*

Let's start this practice by sitting in a comfortable, upright position on your chair, and placing both feet flat on the floor, about a shoulder-width apart. . .

If you like, you can close your eyes, and then just focus your awareness into your body. Notice how it feels being seated here, with your feet flat on the floor . . . grounded . . . rooted . . . and stable. . .

Now, try to settle your focus onto the flow of your breathing in and out. When you're ready, try easing your breath into a rhythm that's slightly deeper and slower than you would normally use. Notice the feeling of your body slowing down. If you like, you can relax your facial muscles into a warm, friendly expression.

As we go through, you may notice that your mind gets distracted, or starts to wander off, which is totally normal. It's what minds do, and when you notice it happening, you can bring a wise awareness to that, and gently bring your attention back to the focus of this exercise.

We are now going to try to imagine an image of ourselves at our compassionate best: an image of your ideal Compassionate Self, with the qualities that you would like this self to have. Remember, it's not important if it doesn't feel like these are your qualities in your day-to-day life. At the moment, all we are doing is just imagining it; just trying it out. That's all that matters.

Now we're going to focus on the three specific qualities of compassion, one after the other. As we go through each one, we're going to try to get a sense of how each quality is expressed in the image of your Compassionate Self.

So, let's start with *caring-commitment*. Your ideal Compassionate Self has a genuine desire and motivation to be helpful and caring in the world. Really try to focus on how that caring quality and intention comes across in your image. Perhaps through body language, facial expression, or some other physical characteristic?

Now let's focus on *wisdom*. Your Compassionate Self is wise and has a deep understanding about the struggles of life. It understands that the brains we have evolved are really tricky for us, and that's not our fault. Just notice for a while how that wisdom is expressed in the image of your Compassionate Self.

And finally, *strength*. Your Compassionate Self has a real calm strength about them which makes them confident in their ability to be caring. Just focus on that quality of strength and see how it shows up in the image.

Okay, so now – just like an actor taking on a role in a film – imagine stepping into the shoes of your Compassionate Self. Really try to feel your way into the body of this character, noticing what it feels like to have these compassionate qualities. What does it feel like to have that caring motivation? What does it feel like having that wise understanding? And where do you feel that strength? Really see if you're able to feel that now in your body: that inner calmness and strength.

Whenever you're ready, we can finish up this exercise. Just check back in with your soothing breathing rhythm, your stable body posture and, in your own time, open your eyes.

––––––

You can hear the audio recording of this exercise on: www.relatingto voices.com/audios

If you need a bit of time to think about how this exercise made you feel, please take that time, and join us back here whenever you're ready.

PRACTICAL BOX

EXERCISE: Your Compassionate Self (embodiment)*

For this exercise, we're going to start off by sitting in a comfortable upright position, with your feet flat on the floor. Just noticing that feeling of connection and stability, here in this chair, here in this moment.

If it feels okay, just close your eyes and try to settle your attention onto the flow of your breathing, in . . . and out. . .

Whenever you're ready, start to bring your mind back to the image of your ideal Compassionate Self, with its qualities of wisdom, strength, and a deep commitment to caring.

Once you feel connected to the image of your Compassionate Self, try to imagine that you are looking at it moving around in the world. Notice your body language and facial expressions when you are embodying your Compassionate Self, and how you interact with other people in your environment. Spend a minute or two just enjoying watching yourself as you go about your day as your Compassionate Self. Try to pay attention to how you relate to other people, and how other people relate to you.

Okay, so in a minute, we're going to be giving this Compassionate Self a bit of a test drive. Imagine that you're an actor who has been studying the character they are about to play. You are now trying to feel your way into the shoes of this character, ready to become your Compassionate Self. Try to connect with what these qualities feel like in your body: the strength, the wisdom, and the desire to be helpful.

When you're ready, you're going to open your eyes and then stand up from your chair in the body and mind of your Compassionate Self. Try to connect with that body posture, that facial expression, and that voice tone, then get up and go for a walk as your ideal Compassionate Self.

We'll see you back here in 5 or 10 minutes, or as many minutes as you need to try this out!

———

You can hear the audio recording of this exercise on: www.relatingto voices.com/audios

If you need a bit of time to think about how this exercise made you feel, please take that time, and join us back here whenever you're ready.

Welcome back to the book! How did your test drive go? Don't worry if that felt a bit strange. It's probably not something you're invited to do every day! However, we do hope that this is something you'll consider bringing into your life more often. You can brush your teeth as your Compassionate Self, you can catch the bus as your Compassionate Self, you can say "good morning" to your neighbour as your Compassionate Self. It really is true that the more we practice, the more natural, easy, and automatic these things become.

The Compassionate Self is essentially a form of identity – a part of ourselves – that holds together a lot of different qualities, processes, physical characteristics, and skills (please see the diagram). In that sense, it acts like a bit of an internal glue for us, in that it holds various things together. This makes the Compassionate Self an important resource when it comes to using compassion in our lives. For example, if we are in a distressing situation, imagine if we had to remember a whole list of helpful qualities, postures, and skills right there on the spot. It would be impossible. Our threat system wouldn't even allow our mind enough time and mental energy to remember all the things that could be helpful in this moment of distress. Instead, it is much easier to call upon a self-identity that we have been training up and practicing. In the moment of distress, we can instead ask ourselves, "**what would my Compassionate Self do in this situation?**" Then immediately we are re-connected to all the postures, qualities, and ways of being in the world that we have linked up with the Compassionate Self. It's the same if we are struggling with voices. For example, we might find ourselves in a situation where we are fighting with voices or being insulted by voices. In that moment, our threat system is highly activated, and we are focused on protecting ourselves. In that moment, we can check in with "**how would my Compassionate Self show up in this moment?**" How would it show up for me? How would it show up for the voice? How would it show up for our relationship?

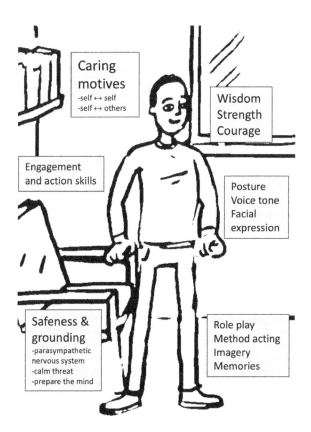

A compassionate self-identity

Image adapted with permission from the online video, "Compassion for Voices: A tale of courage and hope" [29].

Another thing you might want to do is train up different qualities of your Compassionate Self at different times. So, for example, if your voices are being particularly loud and threatening, you may want to spend more time training up the strength and courage qualities of your Compassionate Self. There are various ways of doing this. For instance, strength can be trained up by practicing certain body postures (like the exercise in Chapter 3). There are also a number of imagery exercises that are good for strength (such as images of tall mountains, or ancient trees with their roots going deep into the ground) then imagining that your body is like that mountain or tree. You might go one step further and imagine that your voices are like the weather swirling around the mountain or tree: in other words, focusing on how the inner core stays strong and solid, even though the weather can get quite disruptive. Another helpful approach is using some ideas from martial arts, which are good for helping to train posture and balance. Some CFT colleagues in the UK, Syd Hiskey and Neil Clapton, have been looking closely at the many things martial arts can offer in compassion training [30].

Your ideal compassionate other

There may also be times where we could do with the support and presence of a caring outsider – especially if we are struggling to find our own compassionate wisdom and strength in our relationship with our voices. Developing an image of an ideal compassionate "other" could either be used together with our own Compassionate Self or it could be used instead of it (particularly at first). This can be especially helpful if we are still struggling to connect with, or act in the shoes of, our own Compassionate Self. In this section, we will firstly create a list of the ideal characteristics of our Compassionate Other, and then we will do an imagery practice where this ideal Compassionate Other *comes alongside* you to help you with building up your compassionate qualities. So, in this practice, the Compassionate Other will be supporting you as you connect with your Compassionate Self and try to develop its strength, wisdom, and caring-commitment.

PRACTICAL BOX

EXERCISE: A profile of your ideal Compassionate Other

What would your ideal Compassionate Other look like? Would it be human or non-human? (for example, it could be a human, an animal, or something in nature, like a tree or the ocean)

. . . .

. . . .

What are the physical characteristics of your ideal Compassionate Other? (for example, if it has a face, what sort of expression does it have? If it can speak, what would its voice sound like?)

. . . .

. . . .

How would your ideal Compassionate Other show their compassion towards you?

. . . .

. . . .

How would it feel to be in the presence of your ideal Compassionate Other?

. . . .

. . . .

If you like drawing, maybe you could use this space to draw your Compassionate Other for yourself

A non-human Compassionate Other

PRACTICAL BOX

EXERCISE: Your ideal Compassionate Other supporting your Compassionate Self*

First of all, let's start this exercise by sitting in a comfortable, upright position on your chair then placing both feet flat on the floor, about a shoulder-width apart. . .

If you like, you can close your eyes then just focus your awareness into your body. Just notice how it feels to be seated here like this with your feet flat on the floor . . . grounded . . . rooted . . . and stable. . .

Now, try settling your focus onto the flow of your breath in and out. When you're ready, ease the rhythm of your breathing slightly deeper and slower than you normally would. Take a moment to notice the feeling of your body slowing down. If you like, you can relax your facial muscles into a warm, friendly expression.

And as we go through this exercise, you may notice that your mind gets distracted, or starts to wander off. This is totally normal – it's what minds do. Whenever you notice it happening, just gently bring your attention back to the focus of this exercise.

We are now going to bring to mind an image of your ideal Compassionate Other. This is a supportive other who is deeply caring and committed to looking after you. This ideal Compassionate Other is wise, strong, and genuinely wants to help, so just spend a minute focusing on what your image looks like. Imagine how the compassionate qualities are conveyed in this image: the wisdom, the strength, and the caring.

Now, imagine that this ideal Compassionate Other is beside you, at your shoulder or as close by as is comfortable. Notice how it feels to be there in the presence of this supportive other.

The Compassionate Other wants to help you develop your compassionate wisdom and strength. And it will be there for you, guiding you with that, by providing wisdom and strength for you to draw upon.

Notice what it feels like to develop your Compassionate Self with the support of your ideal Compassionate Other. Building these qualities, sharing them together, and then really feeling those qualities in your body.

Okay, so now just check back in with your soothing breathing rhythm, your stable body posture, and, when you're ready, finishing the exercise and opening your eyes.

––––––

You can hear the audio recording of this exercise on: www.relatingto voices.com/audios

If you need a bit of time to think about how this exercise made you feel, please take that time, and join us back here whenever you're ready.

Compassionate Mind Training

Compassionate Mind Training (CMT) is an important part of CFT. There is now a lot of evidence to show that our brains can be trained, re-shaped, and re-patterned throughout our lives. Our brain's amazing ability to do this is called *neuroplasticity* and it refers to how we can form new connections as a result of new experiences and training. This means our brain's structure is never set in one fixed way; instead, it is constantly growing and adapting to new experiences.

Neuroplasticity is a key principle behind the importance of CMT. For example, some early research involved putting London taxi drivers into brain scanners [31]. The results showed that the drivers' brains were physically different to the brains of non-taxi drivers. In particular, the drivers had an enlarged hippocampus, which is the area of the brain that helps us with navigation and memorising locations. This study demonstrated that repeated practice with using the brain in a particular way (in this case, driving a taxi) actually *shapes* the brain. So, if it works for driving taxis, why not for compassion training? In fact, researchers have investigated just that, by putting people in brain scanners to measure what effect compassionate activities have on the brain. In 2013, researchers in the USA found that two weeks of compassion training led to increased acts of kindness and to changes in brain areas linked with our ability to manage emotions and to interact in our social lives [32]. In turn, researchers in Germany found that one day of compassion training led to changes in the brain areas linked to relationships and positive emotion [33]. Of course, for most of us it will take longer than a few weeks to see results – especially if our brains have already been extensively shaped by a lot of negative experiences – so please don't feel discouraged if it takes a while to feel any improvement. However, findings like this are very hopeful and empowering because they show that the way we think and feel about ourselves and the world is not set in stone. With the right amount of time and practice, even responses that seem very ingrained and automatic can slowly start to change into something more peaceful and helpful.

The three flows of compassion

Within this approach, CMT aims to practice developing something called "the three flows of compassion": 1) self-to-other (compassion flowing from you to other people), 2) other-to-self (receiving compassion from others), and 3) self-to-self (compassion for yourself). There are several different exercises that we use to train up each of these flows. One of us (Charlie) developed an eight-week CMT course for the general public with a colleague, Chris Irons, which has been running in the UK since 2016 by the CFT organisation, Balanced Minds. In an evaluation of 55 people who attended the initial courses in London, we found that CMT led to improvements on outcomes such as compassion, self-reassurance, emotional well-being, self-criticism, stress, and depression [34]. These courses focus on training each of three flows of compassion, and helping people with the fears, blocks, and resistances that arise in each of them. We will come back to some of the common fears of compassion in the following in this section, "*Why is compassion difficult? And what can we do about it?*", after we have spent a bit of time developing your own personal CMT plan.

Your Compassionate Mind Training plan

Imagine that your Compassionate Self (or Compassionate Other) is now taking the role of your coach or personal trainer. In the same way that people have personal trainers for their physical fitness and health, your Compassionate Self will now become your personal trainer for your mental health. For physical fitness, a personal trainer usually sets out a weekly training plan (Monday: working on your calf muscles, Tuesday: cardio training, Wednesday: working on your abs, and so on). In the next exercise, your Compassionate Self (or your Compassionate Other, if you prefer) is going to set out a Compassionate Mind Training plan for you over the next week. We have given you a few suggestions of the kinds of things that other people have in their training plans, so feel free to use some of these ideas, or come up with your own.

PRACTICAL BOX

EXERCISE: My Compassionate Mind Training plan

You can start off by sitting with your feet on the floor in a calm, settled body posture and then just noticing the feeling of stability in your body. Now, bring your attention to the breath, and settle into your soothing breathing rhythm.

When you're ready, bring to mind the image of your Compassionate Self, doing your best to focus on the qualities of wisdom, strength, and caring-commitment. As much as you can, try to step into the shoes of your Compassionate Self, and connect with these qualities in yourself.

Now, as your Compassionate Self, imagine you are in the role of a compassionate coach, and you want to come up with a training plan to help you bring more compassion into your life.

Begin by focusing on the week ahead, and keeping in mind the three flows of compassion (showing compassion to others, allowing yourself to accept compassion from others, and showing compassion to yourself) begin writing your training plan in the following diary:

	Mon	Tue	Wed	Thu	Fri	Sat	Sun
CMT plan							
Notes							

Okay, great. Thank you for doing that – and good luck! There is a space to write a few notes as well, as you go through the week. These could be any reflections, observations, or difficulties that come up; or anything at all really, from either you or your voices.

Why is compassion difficult? And what can we do about it?

Why is compassion difficult?

There have already been a couple of times in the book where we highlighted how these exercises can sometimes activate our threat system – and that this is entirely understandable. It doesn't mean that we're doing anything wrong, or that we should stop doing the exercises all together. Working with our threat system is just a normal part of the process on our journey to compassion. You're doing this journey together with your threat system. The two of you are partners and you can help each other out. Remember that your threat system is only trying to protect you. It can be a very over-enthusiastic protector at times (like the over-sensitive smoke detector in Chapter 2, which goes off even when we've burnt the toast!) but at the end of the day, we can benefit greatly by having this built-in alert system of ours. So, what are some of the things that might activate the threat system when it comes to compassion?

In Chapter 3, we described how safeness can activate threat, at least to begin with (page 46). Later in that chapter, we described how social connection and closeness can also activate threat for some people (page 58). So, as CMT often involves one or both of these things, they can be part of what people's threat systems are reacting to. There are also a number of other common fears that can be triggered by compassion. For example, some people might fear that compassion is weak or self-indulgent. For others, compassion might activate feelings of grief or sadness to do with their past (for example, we might feel upset that we never experienced compassion when we were growing up). For many people, self-criticism can get in the way of compassion, whereas for others it may be that their voices create barriers which make compassion difficult. When this happens, it is sometimes because compassion has been connected with a threat at some point, or perhaps been linked to painful memories. For example, this may have happened when other people harmed us, especially if they should have been caring (such as our parents or teachers), or if they pretended to be caring before causing us harm.

Fears of compassion are very common. In fact, they're so common that there is even a questionnaire that measures them called the *Fears of Compassion Scales* [35]. This questionnaire is divided into three parts, one for each of the three flows of compassion (self-to-other, other-to-self, and self-to-self). It is important to think in terms of the different flows here because there could be very different fears of *giving* compassion than there are for *receiving* compassion. Some people might find giving compassion to others very easy, but when it comes to receiving compassion from others, they find this incredibly hard – or even try to avoid it entirely. (Does this sound familiar to anyone?!). And often, when it comes to self-compassion, some people can find this the hardest flow of all.

What can we do about it?

Given that fears of compassion are such a common part of the process, we will spend the rest of this chapter focusing on some ideas that might help you make sense of these fears as you start your Compassionate Mind Training plan. The first thing is to try and get an understanding of what the fear is about. What is your threat system saying? Why has it popped up? Sometimes it can be very clear what the fear is, but other times not so clear. If it is not obvious, one suggestion would be to just run through the *Fears of Compassion Scales* for yourself. The questionnaire is freely available to access from the Compassionate Mind Foundation website (www.compassionatemind.co.uk/resource/scales). All you have to do is to go through and score yourself on a scale of 0–4 for each statement: 10 statements for self-to-other compassion, 13 for other-to-self, and 15 for self-to-self. Most people find some statements which apply to them, and the ones where you're scoring higher (3s and 4s) are likely to be the fears that apply to you the most. Being aware of this can be a really helpful guide for you to use as you move forward with bringing compassion into your life.

The next thing to do is to be compassionate towards the fact that you are struggling with compassion! (To be honest, it took us a while to get our heads around that!). What this means is recognising that our struggle with compassion is not our fault. It's understandable with this tricky brain of ours. And many other people struggle with it too, just like us. Compassion is hard. This is not only because of the design of our tricky brain (with its natural preference for threat) but is also due to how our brains have become shaped and patterned by our past experiences and relationships. It's not our fault, but we do have choices, and we can take actions to start shaping our brains for the future (through training and *neuroplasticity*, as described earlier). So, please try to be compassionate towards your struggles with compassion. Try to bring empathy and support to yourself with these struggles, and don't forget how normal and common they are. And then, after that, try to develop a compassionate action to help you work your way through and then overcome these struggles.

Overcoming our fears of compassion involves the same process as overcoming any fear. The process is usually a gradual (step-by-step) exposure to what's scaring us. So, with other fears (for example, a fear of spiders, flying, or leaving the house), the typical way we would set out to overcome them would be gradual exposure to the thing we fear. This would happen in steps, so let's use a fear of spiders as an example. For Step 1, we might start by looking at a photograph of a spider; for Step 2, we might hold a cuddly toy spider; for Step 3, we might be in the same room as a real spider, and so on. People using this technique can eventually get to the point where they could hold a real spider in their hand and not feel any fear at all. The idea is that we are building up gradual steps so that the fear never becomes too much to deal with. Each time we take a step, we feel anxiety in our body, but we learn that it's okay and that we can manage it. Over time, we get better and better at tolerating the anxious feeling, and the same is true of a fear of compassion. Just like any fear, a fear of compassion can be addressed by taking it step-by-step: not too fast, not too slow, but learning that it's okay and allowing our body to get used to the feelings. Of course, we must try to be compassionate with ourselves during this process and use our Compassionate Self qualities of wisdom and strength. The wisdom might help us to not go too fast; the strength/courage might help us to not go too slow. Just take care of yourself and stay connected as best you can with that motivation and intention to help.

Remember that, if needed, we also have all the resources we learnt about in Chapter 3. So, if at any time the threat gets too much, or feels too overwhelming, we know how to activate our soothing system (such as using our breathing rhythm, body postures, and imagery). At this point, it might be helpful to remind yourself about what you put into your "safety and safeness kit" on page 61. Safety and safeness are always there as a place to come back to.

There is also a resource developed by CFT colleagues called "The Compassionate Ladder" [36] (please see resource box), which might be a useful tool for you when guiding yourself forwards with practicing compassion. The idea of the ladder is that there is always somewhere to go – you never get "trapped" in one place. If you have gone up a step and find that your threat system has become triggered, then you can always come down the rungs of the ladder to other exercises that feel easier (such as soothing breathing, calm place, and posture). And then, when you are feeling safer, you can step back up the rungs again.

RESOURCE BOX

DIAGRAM: The Compassionate Ladder

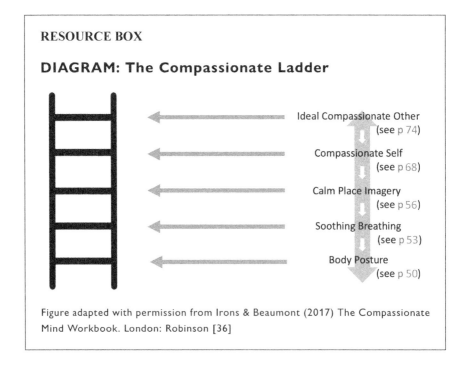

Ideal Compassionate Other
(see p 74)

Compassionate Self
(see p 68)

Calm Place Imagery
(see p 56)

Soothing Breathing
(see p 53)

Body Posture
(see p 50)

Figure adapted with permission from Irons & Beaumont (2017) The Compassionate Mind Workbook. London: Robinson [36]

Taking your Compassionate Self forward in this book

We have now come to the end of Part 2. This means that we now have all the resources we need to take into Part 3, which is when we will be putting these resources to work. The Compassionate Self will be the basis from which we will be relating to yourself and your emotions (Chapter 5), understanding your voices (Chapter 6), and relating to your voices (Chapter 7). Remember that just like the runner who trains before a marathon, the Compassionate Self can also benefit from training, because it takes courage to relate to difficult experiences in a compassionate way. Now that we have developed a Compassionate Self in this chapter, we will start to include this into your check-in boxes as well. This will give you some practice of showing up for yourself, your emotions, and your voices with compassion. There will be plenty more guidance on specific ways to do this in Part 3, but just for now, before you read on, we thought it would be good to have a quick go at this based on the knowledge and resources that you have developed so far in this book. So, we'd like to invite you to have a quick compassionate check-in with yourself, using this check-in box, and we look forward to seeing you again in Part 3!

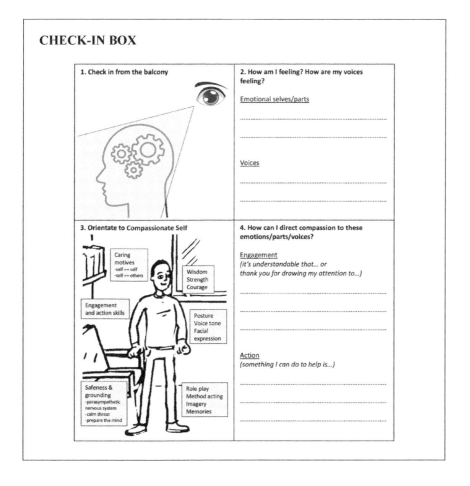

CHECK-IN BOX

1. Check in from the balcony

2. How am I feeling? How are my voices feeling?

Emotional selves/parts

Voices

3. Orientate to Compassionate Self

Caring motives
-self ↔ self
-self ↔ others

Wisdom
Strength
Courage

Engagement and action skills

Posture
Voice tone
Facial expression

Safeness & grounding
-parasympathetic nervous system
-calm threat
-prepare the mind

Role play
Method acting
Imagery
Memories

4. How can I direct compassion to these emotions/parts/voices?

Engagement
(it's understandable that... or thank you for drawing my attention to...)

Action
(something I can do to help is...)

Part 3

The courage of compassionate relating

Chapter 5

Relating compassionately to yourself and your emotions

Chapter summary

How do we think, feel, and behave towards ourselves when we are struggling?

This chapter will focus on the importance of our relationship with ourselves when we're going through a difficult time. Firstly, we will think about how we typically act towards ourselves when we're struggling. We will then move on to consider ways of showing up to support ourselves with compassion – or, in other words, showing up for ourselves as our Compassionate Self.

In this chapter, we will also begin to put our Compassionate Self to work in a number of different ways, including:

- relating to our emotions
- working with self-criticism
- taking care of ourselves in difficult situations.

Introduction

Struggling with our voices is hard enough as it is – but what often makes things even harder is the way we treat ourselves when we're struggling. For many of us, this can often end up bringing a whole layer of additional struggle on top. In CFT language, we can think of this as a *threat about threat*. We will begin this topic by considering our relationship with ourselves more generally, and then spend some time paying closer attention to some of the subtle differences in how we might relate to different *parts* of us: particularly our emotions and vulnerabilities.

How are we with ourselves generally?

"Get a grip of yourself!"
"For goodness' sake, sort it out!"
"What's the matter with you? Can't you do anything right?"

Does this sound familiar to you? For some of us, this might bring back memories of how a critical teacher or parent used to speak to us when we were a child.

DOI: 10.4324/9781003166269-8

However, what we might be less aware of is that many of us have adopted a similar style of relating to ourselves. Psychologists sometimes call this "internalisation", and it basically means that certain messages from the outside can end up becoming a part of us – often without us even noticing we're doing it. And even if we *do* notice a critical style in how we think about ourselves, we might not have considered whether there are any alternatives to this. Instead, we may have just accepted that this is how it is, rather than something we can learn to have control over.

If you would like to (and it's totally up to you, of course), you could maybe just pause for a minute and think about this question for yourself before reading on: *When things go wrong for me, how do I react towards myself?*

People have many different ways of relating to themselves. For example, Paul Gilbert and colleagues developed a questionnaire to measure different forms of self-criticism and self-reassurance, in which they separated self-criticism into two main categories: "inadequate self" and "hated self" [37]. The "inadequate self" category includes statements like:

- "I am easily disappointed in myself".
- "I remember and dwell on my failings".

While the "hated self" category includes statements like:

- "I have become so angry with myself that I want to hurt or injure myself".
- "I do not like being me".

For many of us, these different ways of relating to ourselves can have a significant impact; not least because they are filled with negative emotions, ranging from disappointment and frustration to outright rage and hostility. Not only can this affect our mood, but it can also create different responses in our bodies and an urge to act in certain ways. In this respect, brain scan research has shown that responding to ourselves in ways that are critical activate very different patterns in our brains compared to responses that are reassuring [38]. With such powerful influences, it's no wonder that the way we respond to ourselves can make our existing emotional and mental health struggles feel so much worse. It's as if we "feel bad about feeling bad". And of course, it's often at the times when we're struggling the most that our self-criticism has the most powerful influence.

We will return to self-criticism, and working with self-criticism, later on in the chapter. For now, we will instead turn to thinking about the types of relationship we have with different parts of ourselves, as well as with our different emotions.

How are we with the parts of us, and the emotions, that we find most difficult?

Just as we might relate to different parts of our bodies in different ways (for example, a person might like the colour of their eyes, but can't stand the shape of their nose), we can also have different relationships with certain emotions and parts of our identity. Some people particularly can't bear emotions that make them feel most vulnerable, probably because vulnerability is a threat to our natural survival instincts. For example, if the emotion of sadness makes us feel low and vulnerable, then we might try to prevent or block that feeling from being expressed (or even experienced). We might fear that if people saw it then they could hurt us or take advantage of us. Of course, if this is something that has happened to you in the past (for example, if you have childhood memories of feeling sad and being told "don't be so pathetic"), then you might have – very understandably – learned to fear and avoid the emotion of sadness. This is one example, but there can be many other types of fears related to other emotions. With anger, for instance, some of the fears might be less about vulnerability and more about confrontation or conflict. Consider someone who was always punished as a child for showing anger; they may find themselves growing up feeling very fearful of what could happen if they lose their temper. They may even be afraid of trying to stand up for themselves and be assertive due to a belief that something bad could happen if they do. Other people talk about fearing joy and happiness, often saying that, for them, happiness brings an anticipation of getting hurt if someone takes it away or it ends.

Everyone has different versions of this. There is no right or wrong, we've just all had different experiences that have led to have different types of relationships with our feelings. Here are some examples of ways that people might relate to difficult emotions and vulnerabilities:

> Dan is **afraid of** becoming anxious in his job interview tomorrow.
>
> Faiza is **afraid of** talking about the loss of her brother for **fear of** becoming overwhelmed by sadness.
>
> Hakeem and Shelley are both **afraid of** conflict, so have learnt to **avoid and hide** their anger.
>
> Tina is **ashamed of** what happened to her in the past, when she was vulnerable or hurt as a child.
>
> Greg is **ashamed about** being seen as vulnerable by others if he's "too emotional".
>
> Khadija, who has been diagnosed with depression, is **afraid and ashamed of** her emotions as being a sign or "symptom" of her mental health difficulties getting worse.

In these examples, the words in **bold** all relate to secondary reactions that happen in response to a primary problem: for example, being afraid of an emotional experience (fear, sadness, and anger) or feeling ashamed of vulnerability. In that sense, these are all examples of a "struggle with a struggle" (or a "threat about threat"). In other words, these are to do with the relationship someone has with their struggle, rather than the struggle itself. Does that make sense? In the remainder of this chapter, we will try and address this idea of a "struggle with a struggle" because it potentially has a lot to answer for in keeping people trapped in patterns of difficulty with their mental health. And, as we talked about earlier, it's often when we are struggling the most with our voices and mental health that these emotional conflicts and patterns become the strongest. It's during these times, more than ever, that we need to show up for ourselves with compassionate intentions, wisdom, and care.

Setting up relationships with our emotional parts

In Chapter 2, we did an exercise focusing on the three emotions of anger, anxiety, and sadness as "parts" of us. It was as if each of them was a separate character with its own sets of motives, thoughts, ways of paying attention, behaving, and so on. We spent a bit of time getting to know your angry self, your anxious self, and your sad self. (If you want to refer back to this, it was called "multiple selves" on page 34). A very good example of characterising these emotions as different selves comes from the 2015 Disney Pixar movie, *Inside Out*. There is one particular scene called the "Family Dinner scene" (it's a 3-minute clip which you can easily find on YouTube), which is really worth watching as it shows the multiple selves in action for each person (mum, dad, and daughter) as they sit around the dinner table. Do you notice any similarities between their multiple selves and your own multiple selves on page 34?

One of the important things to notice about our multiple selves is that whichever part/self is active will be the one that fills our attention and creates different thoughts, urges, and responses. We might have also noticed that we can shift attention between the various selves. This, in itself, is a helpful thing to recognise and remember; the fact that we can *choose* to switch attention between these parts of us. Those of you who have any experience of mindfulness will know that attention, and the ways we choose to pay attention, is a powerful tool that we can all learn and train. (We talked about mindfulness briefly on page 68). Mindfulness practice can be very useful when it comes to dealing with our multiple selves and developing more compassionate ways of relating to ourselves when we're struggling.

Another important thing about seeing our emotions as multiple selves is that, in a way, it makes them easier to understand and relate to. Again, this is what the filmmakers did so well in *Inside Out* because the audience really got to *know* these characters (Anger, Fear, Sadness, Joy, and Disgust) and their personalities. This can help create a bit of a shift for us: away from "experiencing an emotion" and more towards "being in a relationship with an emotion". For example, with the emotion of anxiety, this shift might be away from "I am feeling anxious" and more towards "my anxious self has come online" or "the anxious part of me is saying/feeling/ wanting to . . .". This immediately sets up the opportunity for a different way of relating to our anxiety. Rather than experiencing it as something all-consuming, which can lead to us feeling overwhelmed (and more anxious), the emotion is now experienced as something we can be in a relationship with. It helps us to recognise that although we may be feeling anxious, it's only one part of us – and that there are many other parts as well. Rather than "I AM anxious" (i.e. my anxiety defines me) we can think "My anxious self is very active right now" (i.e. "although my anxiety is powerful, it has not taken over – I'm still here too"). With this slight distancing, we might now have access to different choices. For example, we might start to be a bit more curious about this anxious part of ourselves. We might want to learn a bit more about this self/character, and what it's concerned about. In the long term, this can be very helpful, because if we can understand this part of ourselves more clearly, then ultimately, we can learn how to try to help it out.

We also mentioned on page 36 that it can be useful to consider the different relationships we have with each of our multiple selves. As you may remember, CFT does not focus so much on joy and disgust, but instead emphasises anger, anxiety (fear), and sadness, because these are the three emotions which cause us to struggle the most with our mental health. Which of these three selves – angry, anxious, and sad – do you find easiest to access? Which of them do you find hardest to access? Keeping this in mind, we now want to invite you to create a map that visually shows your relationship with your own multiple selves. In the practical box, we have described an exercise that should help you to make a start on doing this.

PRACTICAL BOX

EXERCISE: Mapping your multiple selves

The example of John.

This is an example map which shows the three different emotional selves, and the relationships John has with them. John's anxious self is drawn as being very close, which represents how this emotion feels very present and easy to access. On the other hand, sad self is drawn further away, which represents how this emotion is more cut off from his day-to-day experience. This means that while John can find himself growing anxious or angry fairly quickly in response to a threat, he does not want to allow himself to feel sadness and keeps these feelings pushed away.

Use this space to map out your own multiple selves, and your relationships with each:

Showing up for our emotions with compassion

Once we've mapped out the parts and discovered a bit more about them and how they affect us, we can begin thinking about the type of relationship we *want* to develop towards them – particularly, those parts with which we are struggling the most. This is where we bring in our Compassionate Self. In Chapter 4, we learnt that the Compassionate Self is essentially a part of ourselves (sometimes called a "self-identity") that connects with our most wise, caring, and courageous qualities. Showing up for ourselves from a place of compassion can potentially really help with this issue of the "struggle with a struggle" that we talked about earlier. Remember how we talked about the secondary layer of struggle – that sense of "feeling bad about feeling bad"? Well, if we are able to reduce that then we might find that we are in a better position to deal with the struggle itself.

To help guide us through the process of showing up as our Compassionate Self, we're going to use the example of the anxious self as the part we want to help. But before we do that, let's just remind ourselves of the definition of compassion that we use in CFT: "*a sensitivity to suffering in ourselves and others, with a commitment to try to reduce and prevent it*". So, applying this definition to the case of our anxious self, compassion might firstly involve:

- a sensitive *engagement* with the distress of the anxious self (for example, listening to it, showing it empathy, taking its concerns seriously, and courageously standing alongside it in its struggles), and then
- to approach that struggle by learning what is helpful and taking compassionate *action*.

The first part, or what we would call the *compassionate engagement* part, might involve listening to what the anxious self is saying, and really noticing where that shows up in the body.

Think?	*"I can't cope"; "This is all going to go wrong"*
Feel?	*Feelings are showing up in the pit of my stomach and a racing heartbeat*
Want to do?	*Run away, get out of here*
Memories?	*That time I was really anxious at school, and everyone laughed at me*

Then, for the second stage, which we would call the *compassionate action* stage, we want to draw on our wisdom to think about which qualities, skills, and responses would be most helpful for the anxious self to start feeling better. For example, qualities such as calmness and a non-judgemental attitude might be helpful, as might skills such as grounding exercises, mindfulness, and deep breathing. Then, after that, our compassionate action might be to respond to our anxious self, with either a spoken or written response. Here is an example of how a letter might start off, written from the Compassionate Self to the anxious self:

Dear anxious self,

Thank you for showing up for me today. I can understand why you're here; I know it's because you are doing your job for me, like you always have done – the job that only you know how to do best. Your job is to warn me of any danger or potential threat. You know what my greatest fears are: you've studied and learnt these throughout my whole life, and you've remembered all the times in my life when I've been in danger or been afraid.

This must be really hard for you right now, having these thoughts of not being able to cope, and imagining all the things that could go wrong. I can understand why you're worried about these things because there have been times in the past, particularly at school, where things really did get tough. I know you're working so hard for me to keep me safe from things like this happening again. I really want to try and help, and I hope that we can work on some of these fears and memories together. I'm right here with you, I'm alongside you, I can understand how you feel.

We can work on this together as team.

The letter might then go on to suggest some ideas and strategies for things that can help to settle the anxious feelings in the body: for example, suggestions for getting grounded and practicing soothing breathing exercises. The Compassionate Self might try to reassure the anxious self that, while in the memories of school, there really were threatening/humiliating experiences surrounding these anxious feelings, these are not happening now and these memories belong to the past, not the present. Potentially the Compassionate Self can tell anxious self things like: "you are safe now", "I'm not going to judge you", "I'm here to help, and I'm staying right here for you as much as you need". Remember too that this is not about trying to solve the *primary* struggle (for example, being worried about a job interview), because when anxious self is very active these kinds of logical arguments will be almost impossible for it to hear. Instead, Compassionate Self is trying to soothe and comfort the *secondary* feelings of fear and shame.

In the following diagram, we have developed our visual map by bringing in a new addition: the Compassionate Self. We have shown how the Compassionate Self can be practiced and trained (shown in the map as getting bigger) before we "become" the Compassionate Self. This means that we step into the shoes of this character and use it as a safe, secure base from which to relate to our emotional selves.

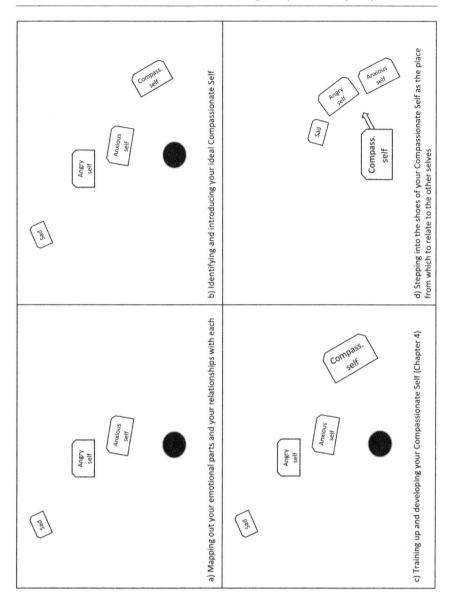

a) Mapping out your emotional parts and your relationships with each

b) Identifying and introducing your ideal Compassionate Self

c) Training up and developing your Compassionate Self (Chapter 4)

d) Stepping into the shoes of your Compassionate Self as the place from which to relate to the other selves

Showing up as your Compassionate Self

Diagram adapted with permission from Heriot-Maitland, C. (2022) in G. Simos & P. Gilbert (Eds.) Compassion Focused Therapy in Clinical Practice. Routledge [39]

Here are two exercises where we can try this idea out directly. In these exercises, we'll invite you to remember the example of the argument from Chapter 2, and to practice showing up as your Compassionate Self for: 1) the argument situation, and then 2) the multiple selves. Whenever you're ready, let's make a start on these together.

PRACTICAL BOX

EXERCISE: Bringing your Compassionate Self to the argument situation

Remember in Chapter 2, when we invited you to think about a recent argument in your life? You pictured the scene in your mind, and then captured what was going on for each of your multiple selves, in terms of its:

•   Thoughts (what's happening in the mind?)
•   Feelings (what's happening in the body?)
•   Behaviour (what does the self have an urge to do?)
•   Outcome (what does the self most want to happen in this situation?)

We will now go back to this argument, but this time as your Compassionate Self.

So, to start off with, let's prepare our body to support our mind. We can do this by getting into an upright, settled body posture with our feet flat on the floor.

When you're ready, close your eyes and just notice how that feels: being grounded, rooted, and stable.

Now, try focusing on the flow of your breathing in and out. Connect with your soothing breathing rhythm and just notice the feeling of your body slowing down.

In your own time, try to bring the qualities of your Compassionate Self into your mind: qualities such as wisdom, strength, and caring-commitment. Just imagine stepping into the shoes of your Compassionate Self and begin to feel your way into these qualities. What that wisdom feels like? What that strength feels like? And really connecting with a genuine desire to be caring and helpful in the world. . .

Okay, so now begin bringing the argument situation back into your mind. Really try to stay anchored in your Compassionate Self as you look at this argument scene through these eyes. And then, whenever you're ready, just go through these four steps:

1.   *Thoughts/mind:* what's going through the mind of your Compassionate Self? What does your Compassionate Self think or understand about this situation?
2.   *Feel/body:* notice what that feels like in your body.

3. *Behaviour/urge:* what does your Compassionate Self want to do?
4. *Preferred outcome:* what does your Compassionate Self want as the outcome?

Once you've had a chance to really focus on this, try writing your responses down here:

Compassionate Self

Thoughts/mind . . . .

Feel/body . . . .

Behaviour/urge . . . .

Preferred outcome. . . . .

Thank you for doing this exercise. What did you notice? What did you learn? Before moving on, it might be helpful to think about whether there are any other situations or difficulties in your life that you might want to use this exercise for.

PRACTICAL BOX

EXERCISE: Bringing the Compassionate Self to your multiple selves

Now that we've had time to think about the actual argument, we're going to focus on how the Compassionate Self might want to show up for each of the multiple selves. Remember that the Compassionate Self has a wise understanding about our tricky brains and the way they have evolved over time to react to things in ways that we did not choose. The Compassionate Self understands, for example, that our threat system does a particular job for us – keeping us safe – and that the emotions of the threat system have specific functions. Likewise, Compassionate Self understands that the angry self is very good at attending to **wrongdoing**, the anxious self is very good at attending to **dangers**, and the sad self is very good at attending to **losses**. So, when we're thinking about our compassionate responses to the different selves, firstly consider the function that each self is performing (left column), before considering your response (right column):

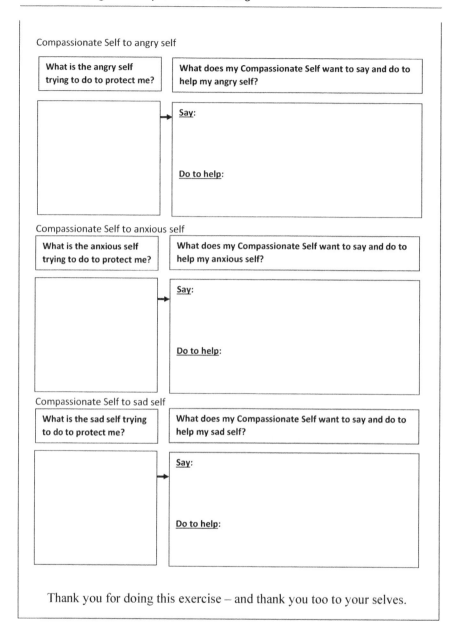

Compassionate Self to angry self

What is the angry self trying to do to protect me?	What does my Compassionate Self want to say and do to help my angry self?
	Say: Do to help:

Compassionate Self to anxious self

What is the anxious self trying to do to protect me?	What does my Compassionate Self want to say and do to help my anxious self?
	Say: Do to help:

Compassionate Self to sad self

What is the sad self trying to do to protect me?	What does my Compassionate Self want to say and do to help my sad self?
	Say: Do to help:

Thank you for doing this exercise – and thank you too to your selves.

Working with self-criticism

At the start of this chapter, we invited you think about the following question: *When things go wrong for you, how do you respond to yourself?* For many of us, we will have noticed that at times like this, and perhaps many other times too, we can be very self-critical. Self-criticism is a common block to self-compassion, so we now want to spend some time focusing on self-criticism: getting to know it a bit more, finding out more about it, and then hopefully identifying some ways in which we might be able to help. As we will discover as we go through this section, our self-criticism often has a function. In the same way that each of our emotional selves have functions, so does our self-critical part (or what we can simply call our "self-critic").

Many of us who grew up around critical adults, such as parents or teachers, are likely to have a very active self-critic because we learnt early on that criticising ourselves was a helpful way to avoid mistakes and make sure these adults didn't become angry with us. We criticised ourselves before anyone else could, and that felt like a useful way of staying safe. As such, we can see that the self-critic is doing a job for us – typically linked to our threat system and underlying fears – and because of that we don't want to just take it away or get rid of it. In fact, if we attempted that, we'd likely be met with a strong threat response. If something has a protective function, the idea of it suddenly being taken away or not being there can be scary. (In many ways, this is similar to critical voices, as we'll explore in the next two chapters). Therefore, rather than trying to ignore or get rid of the self-critic, we will suggest that the Compassionate Self can instead work *with* the self-critic. As we've mentioned before, the CFT approach is all about switching from threat-focused patterns of conflict and competition towards caring-focused patterns of collaboration and co-operation. The same principle applies to working with our own self-critical part.

Let's look a bit closer at the nature of self-criticism with an example from sport:

> It's 05th July 2021 at the Wimbledon tennis tournament, and the British player Emma Raducanu has been forced to retire from her match with Ajla Tomljanovic after experiencing breathing difficulties on court. Her exit is a shock: having risen up the ranks with impressive speed, people were already starting to describe this talented young woman as someone to pay attention to in British tennis. Crashing out of the competition so unexpectedly was extremely disappointing, especially when reports began to circulate that Emma's breathing problems might partly have been caused by anxiety. When asked about it later, Emma simply described how the demands of competing at such a high level may have "caught up with me".

From what we've learnt about our threat system, we could easily imagine that Emma's threat system is starting to accept the possibility of a serious impact on her career. Usually, the threat system anticipates danger and wants to make sure we are prepared. This might well involve imagining the worst-case scenarios in order to prepare us and to lessen our pain (and surprise) if that scenario happens. One thing the threat system really doesn't like is being caught off guard.

If you prepare yourself for failure now, Emma, then the pain of the loss will be easier to bear when it happens. Don't get your hopes up, because if you do and everything goes wrong then that would be doubly painful for you. Remember how disappointing and humiliating it was when the medical team had to take you off the court? Just imagine how you'll feel if that happens again. Think of how negative and mocking the headlines would be. You're not good enough, Emma, you're out of your depth. You should just accept that you're not cut out to compete against the best players in the world.

We are obviously making this up (because we have no access to Emma's mind), but you get the picture! The point is that the threat system is protective. It's protecting us from pain and harm. The self-critical aspect that starts appearing in the earlier example is often based on underlying fears (in this case, fears of failure and rejection). Fortunately, in our example, Emma's threat system was not given too much priority. Instead, she returned to her previous form and just a few months later had a stunning success by winning the US Open – one of the youngest women ever to do so. By striking the right balance between her threat, drive, and soothing systems, Emma was able to take a setback in her stride without allowing it to dominate her moving forwards.

Our threat system – which remember, is only concerned with our protection, not our happiness or mental health – will often resort to putting us down before somebody else does. It encourages us to reject ourselves before we are rejected; defeat ourselves before someone else defeats us, because at least that way then the distress will be more within our control. This is the self-critic. We can perhaps think of it a bit like a *controlled explosion* – we fear there might be an explosion, so our self-critic blows things up first to keep the explosion "in house". This is one way in which our self-critic is trying to be protective, even though there are obviously costs to our mental well-being when we are beating ourselves up. Part of being a professional athlete, like Emma Raducanu, is learning how to manage the critic when it is being unhelpful and not allowing it to have an unnecessary impact on performance. For some of us, this is a harder task than it is for others, but that's not our fault – it's because of our early experiences making us very sensitive to the critic's input. However, with the right amount of practice and patience, we can all learn to have more choice and control over how much our critics are able to influence us.

A number of different functions of self-criticism are listed in a scale developed by Paul Gilbert and colleagues, called *The Functions of Self-Criticizing/Attacking Scale* [37]. Here are a few examples of the statements that appear on the scale. You can maybe put a tick next to any of the ones that apply to you.

I get critical and angry with myself:
- To make sure I keep up my standards.
- To stop myself being happy.
- To show I care about my mistakes.
- Because if I punish myself I feel better.
- To stop me being lazy.
- To harm part of myself.
- To keep myself in check.
- To punish myself for my mistakes.
- To stop me getting overconfident.
- To stop me being angry with others.

- To make me concentrate.
- To gain reassurance from others.
- To prevent future embarrassments.

So how can we work with our self-critic? Before we go into that, we think this might be a good time for a check-in. In our experiences of voice-hearing and working with voice-hearers, many people have talked about there being an overlap between self-critical parts (the self-critic) and voices. So, if you are noticing anything now with your voices, or if your voices want to say anything about this topic, please use the space provided in the check-in box.

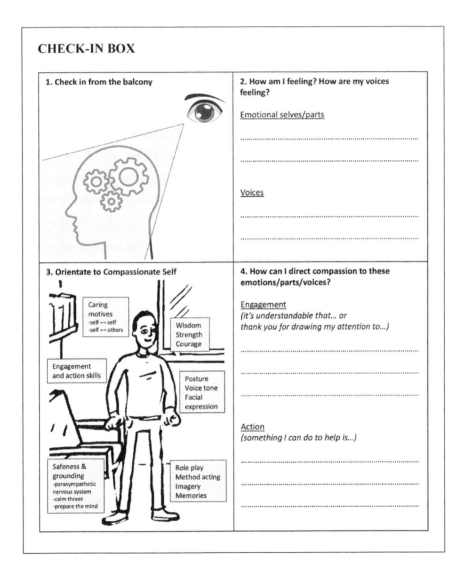

We will now move on to consider how your Compassionate Self can help your self-critic. In attempting this, the first thing we can try to do is to notice when our self-critic is active in the first place. For many people, self-criticism is such an automatic process, and such a natural way of being with themselves, that they don't even realise when they are doing it. So noticing the critic, using that *view from the balcony*, can be a compassionate act in and of itself.

The next thing that the Compassionate Self can do is to develop an understanding of the critic. For example, can the Compassionate Self bring a sense of empathy for why it's there? This is likely to involve developing wisdom about the function of the critic, and about the threat emotions that may be behind it (most commonly fears, vulnerabilities, and insecurities). Some good questions to ask yourself to help you understand the function of the self-critic are:

• How does self-criticism work for me?
• What does it help me do?
• What would be my greatest fear in stopping it or giving it up?

Finally, given what is understood about the function of the critic, the Compassionate Self might then be able to offer to help. For example, if the function of the critic is "to stop me being angry with others", the Compassionate Self might help by practicing assertiveness, so that my needs and boundaries can be communicated to other people in a healthy way. If the function of the critic is "to punish myself for my mistakes", the Compassionate Self might acknowledge the critic's concerns about wanting to make less mistakes and offer to help with a form of self-improvement that is based more on encouragement and support, rather than criticism and punishment. One of the most important things to recognise is that the self-critic and the Compassionate Self often want the same things; however, they go about achieving these things in very different ways.

Using imagery can be another helpful way of getting to know the self-critic and, in time, learning to understand it and develop compassion for it. In the foreword, Paul Gilbert described the use of imagery when working with a self-critic. We won't do this as an exercise here, as we will be doing a similar imagery exercise later in Chapter 7 ("*Compassionate engagement with a voice using imagery*"), which you can also use as a guide for working with self-criticism. However, just to quickly describe how this works: we would usually ask someone to close their eyes and imagine what their self-critic would look like if it was an external being. We often suggest that they don't choose a real person in their life to be the image of their self-critic, and instead use their imagination to visualise the critic standing there in front of them. We would then ask them to notice what the critic looks like, sounds like, to identify the emotions it is directing towards them, and then to notice how it feels to be the target of this criticism. Once someone has an image of their self-critic, they can use imagery to set up a meeting between the Compassionate Self and their self-critic. If you are interested, there is a detailed description of working compassionately with a voice-hearer's self-critic in a recent article called, "A case report of compassion focused therapy for distressing voice-hearing experiences" [11], which is a first-hand account of CFT written by one of us (Charlie) together with a voice-hearer (Valerie).

Showing up for ourselves in day-to-day life

In this chapter, we have been guiding you through different types of self-compassion, with a particular emphasis on how we bring compassion to the parts of us that we struggle with the most, such as our threat-based emotional parts and our self-critical part. However, self-compassion is not only for the parts of us which we experience as being difficult. As we were saying in Chapter 4, we hope that the practice of self-compassion can also be built into your day-to-day Compassionate Mind Training (CMT) and, over time, becomes a more natural way of relating to yourself. Before we finish the chapter, we wanted to give you a couple of practical resources that you can use to bring compassion to yourself more generally during day-to-day situations.

The first exercise is "making a compassionate flashcard". The idea of this is that the card will contain some helpful tips, support, and reminders from your Compassionate Self, which you can then carry round with you and refer to whenever you need it. You can of course design how you'd like your own flashcard, but the way we sometimes like to do it is to make it the size of a credit card so it's easy to fit in a wallet or purse. We then put an image on one side (usually one that is calming or grounding, like a scene from nature, or maybe a pet) and then, on the other side, a collection of supportive words and phrases from our Compassionate Self. In the practical box, we have given some examples that relate to compassionate attention, thinking, and behaviour. However, because so many of the voice-hearers we have met have such creative talents, we don't want to give too many instructions about this – we want you to come up with a design and content that works for you. There will be a place on our website (relatingtovoices.com) where you can send in photos of your own compassionate flashcards, which we hope will become a resource for other voice-hearers. So, time to get creative, and enjoy!

PRACTICAL BOX

EXERCISE: Making a compassionate flashcard

Calming/
  grounding
  image

Compassionate attention

Focus on memories of times I've coped	Notice surroundings / colour
Image of a wise face	Focus on feelings of courage in my body

. . . .

. . . .

Compassionate thinking

Brains are tricky	This too shall pass	You've got this
Anxiety usually peaks then calms in 5 mins		It's not my fault

. . . .

. . . .

Compassionate behaviour

2 mins breathing app	Slow down	Smell my lavender oil
What would my Compassionate Self do?		Listen to music

. . . .

. . . .

Remember to send us your compassionate flashcard creations to the email address: flashcards@relatingtovoices.com

The final two exercises are a bit more experience-based: "A moment of self-C.A.R.E." and "Compassionate Self-to-self using imagery" (both described in the practical boxes). The first one is very short because the idea is that you can use it as a quick, "in the moment", self-compassionate check-in, very similar to the check-in boxes that we have used in this book. The second one is a longer exercise using imagery, for which you may need to set aside about 10 minutes. In this exercise, we get into our Compassionate Self, and then imagine a scene where we are walking down a street in the mind and body of the Compassionate Self. Halfway down the street, we meet with ourselves, and we try to stay with the feelings of this meeting between your Compassionate Self and your (day-to-day) self.

PRACTICAL BOX

EXERCISE: A Moment of Self-C.A.R.E.*

To help us to develop a more compassionate relationship with ourselves, it is very important to keep practicing and repeating the habit of engaging with ourselves in this way. The Moment of Self-C.A.R.E. practice is simple. It involves learning to connect and speak to yourself in a compassionate way. Engaging with ourselves with C.A.R.E involves the following:

C – CONNECT with your Compassionate Self
A – ALLOW yourself to slow down for a moment
R – REFLECT on how you are in this moment
E – EXTEND a sense of care and kindness to yourself

A key part of C.A.R.E. is to check in with ourselves regularly, regardless of how we're feeling. Whether we're happy or sad, excited or anxious, it doesn't matter – we're in training to make a habit of paying kind attention to ourselves, even if it's just for a minute.

When practising C.A.R.E., it might initially be difficult to feel a sense of warmth and kindness, especially in the presence of difficult feelings. This is okay. Self-compassion starts with the intention and motivation to treat yourself in a caring way. The feelings can sometimes lag behind the intent, but with practice, they can grow over time.

Exercise was developed by Chris Irons for the Balanced Minds 8-week CMT course [34].

PRACTICAL BOX

EXERCISE: Compassionate Self-to-self using imagery*

Start off by sitting in a chair in an upright and settled position with your feet flat on the floor. When you're ready, close your eyes and just notice how that feels: to be grounded, rooted, and stable. . .

In your own time, gently bring your focus to the flow of your breathing, in and out, and try to connect with your soothing breathing rhythm. Just notice the feeling of your body slowing down.

Now, if you like, bring a friendly expression to your face, and begin trying to imagine some of the qualities of your ideal Compassionate Self.

First, the quality of **caring motivation**: a deep desire to be kind, caring, and supportive in the world. Imagine having these qualities and how it would feel in your body. What would it be like looking through your eyes with the intention to be caring? Consider what your body posture would be like, what your facial expression would look like, what your voice tone would sound like. . .

Second, consider the quality of **wisdom**: you understand that we have "tricky brains" that were created over millions of years of evolution and which we did not choose for ourselves. You understand that the way our brains make us feel and react is not our fault, but you also know that it is within our power to do something about it. Again, imagine how it would feel to look out through the eyes of your Compassionate Self and have a deep understanding of how hard life can be; to know that all humans face struggles throughout their life which are not their fault.

Finally, consider the quality of **strength and courage**. Just notice how that feels in your body. How would you hold your body? How would you stand with a sense of confidence and strength?

Now, imagine walking down the street as your ideal Compassionate Self with these qualities within you. Really notice how it feels inside of you. Imagine how you would walk and what that feels like. You have a deep intention to be aware of suffering and a desire to try to be supportive and to reduce distress. Imagine being in the body of your Compassionate Self and looking out at the world through that compassionate lens.

Now, as you are walking along, imagine that there in front of you in the street is the image of yourself. This is your everyday self, as you are in the world on a daily basis. Staying anchored in your Compassionate Self, begin to direct this caring motivation towards you. This is someone that you really care about and want to help. . .

From your compassionate wisdom, you know that life can be tough, and people can struggle. Direct that empathy and understanding towards yourself: the awareness that things can be hard for you, and it's not your fault. . .

Now, just spend a minute or two thinking about this meeting between you and your Compassionate Self. Think about how you, as your Compassionate Self, might give this understanding and help to your day-to-day self. Is there anything your Compassionate Self wants to say, or do? And if there is something, what is the voice tone and facial expression that goes along with that supportive message?

(Stay with that for 1–2 minutes)

Okay, when you've done that, you can gradually let the imagery fade away and slowly return your attention to your compassionate qualities. Notice how this feels in your body, your posture, and also in your soothing breathing rhythm. . .

When you're ready to open your eyes, you might want to write down a couple of notes and reflections for yourself about what came up during that meeting between you and your Compassionate Self. . .

(You can use this space here)

. . . .

. . . .

. . . .

. . . .

———

You can hear the audio recording of this exercise on: www.relatingto voices.com/audios

If you need a bit of time to think about how this exercise made you feel, please take that time, and join us back here whenever you're ready.

There are other variations of self-compassion exercises which unfortunately we don't have space to fit in this book. An important one is compassionate letter-writing, but we will guide you through a full letter-writing exercise in Chapter 7 ("*Writing a compassionate letter to a voice*"). Letters can also be written to yourself, or to a part of you which is struggling (for example, the previous letter, when the Compassionate Self was writing to the anxious self). Another exercise to mention that could come into your self-to-self Compassionate Mind Training is "Compassion in the mirror". As you might have guessed, this involves sending compassion to yourself while looking at your reflection in the mirror. Some CFT colleagues in Italy found that when people told themselves compassionate phrases while looking in the mirror, this led to an increased sense of calmness (in other words, their soothing system was activated), and that this was more effective than just saying the words on their own without looking in the mirror [40]. Maybe you could try this using some of the phrases that you came up with for your flashcard?

Of course, it does take effort to continue training and developing your Compassionate Self and, as we discussed in Chapter 4, there are several barriers which we all face in bringing compassion into our daily lives. However, the effort and practice does pay off. According to a study by CFT colleagues in Portugal, the frequency of practicing these exercises was associated with a greater ability to connect with the Compassionate Self, and greater connection was associated with increased compassion, self-reassurance, feelings of safety, and reduced self-criticism [41]. The main message from this chapter is that compassion is something we can *choose* to connect with. So the next time we are struggling with our emotions, vulnerabilities, and our mental health, please try to remember that we have the choice, in that moment, to show up for ourselves with compassion.

Chapter 6

Developing a compassionate understanding of your voices

Chapter summary

Can voices ever be seen as understandable and meaningful in the context of our lives?

In this chapter, we will consider ways of thinking about voices and voice-hearing in terms of our past experiences and relationships. By drawing on the ideas of human development and evolution from the earlier chapters, we will see how understanding voice-hearing as a meaningful response to real-life events and emotions can gradually help us to feel more empowered and less ashamed. After that, we will then begin to explore some of the jobs or functions that our voices may be performing for us. For instance:

- Protecting us from future harm (from others)
- Protecting us from our own difficult feelings and memories
- Drawing our attention to past distress and memories of threat that have not yet been resolved

During this process, we will meet four voice-hearers – Alan, Deepa, Kwame, and Emily – to help illustrate some of these links between voices, the function of voices, and early life experiences. And finally, we will guide you through the process of beginning to develop a compassionate understanding of your own voices.

Introduction

When we defined compassion in Chapter 2, we talked about there being two different aspects: 1) engagement and 2) action. The first, *compassionate engagement*, means acknowledging the suffering and distress of someone or something, then using our empathy to try to understand and make sense of it. The second aspect, *compassionate action*, refers to doing something to help – taking action to help reduce the distress and prevent it from reoccurring in the future. These two aspects of compassion work together, because if we want to reduce suffering and unhappiness, then we need to understand the nature of the distress and what caused it to happen in the first place. Learning to relate compassionately to

DOI: 10.4324/9781003166269-9

distressing voices is no different. Compassionate engagement with voices invites us to try and understand what is *causing* the voices/voice-hearing. Why are the voices there? When and why did they appear, and what events or emotions might be behind them? The beliefs we reach about our voices will have a huge impact on how we relate and respond to them. In other words, our (compassionate) understanding will help us choose what our (compassionate) action is going to be.

Before we get into exploring some ways of understanding voices, we first want to focus on the impact that different types of understanding can have. Some understandings can give us the confidence and motivation to want to help, whereas others can make us feel ashamed or fearful and cause us to avoid the problem. In our experience of mental health services, we have seen the enormous impact that a particular type of understanding can have on people. For example, it is well known that there is big issue with stigma around some of the labels used in the medical model of mental health problems. This means that, for some people, terms like "personality disorder" or "schizophrenia" may sometimes cause more social difficulties in terms of stigma, shame, and employment opportunities, than their actual experience of mental health.

In the medical model of psychosis, voices are referred to as "auditory hallucinations" and often understood to be symptoms of a biological illness called "schizophrenia". So, traditionally, the mainstream understanding has been that voices are caused by an underlying brain disorder. Let's just think about that for a minute. In this understanding, the voices people hear are seen by society as a bad, wrong, or undesirable symptoms of a disordered brain. How do you think that understanding might affect how we relate to our voices? Would it inspire us to listen to them with empathy and patience? To take their concerns seriously and try to care for them? Probably not. More likely it would drive us into an internal battle with our voices by attempting to fight and control them, or to drive them away. In the short term, this angry response might feel helpful, but for many of us, the more angry and rejecting we are to our voices, the more hostile and resentful the voices are towards us. This means that the voices and the voice-hearer can get trapped in a destructive relationship where neither side is able to make peace.

This explains how an understanding can significantly influence our relationship and our response. This is why the understandings we choose form a key part in the compassionate approach, and this chapter will explore the kinds of understandings of voices that can move us away from conflict and towards compassion.

CHECK-IN BOX

How did it feel reading that; the idea of engaging with your voices in a compassionate way? At this point, we thought it was important to acknowledge those of you who might currently feel that your voices are so negative that they don't deserve your compassion. You may have read this paragraph and thought "but my voices are my enemies; I don't *want* to be kind or patient to them". If so, then that's very understandable. It makes sense why you feel that the process we're describing doesn't relate to you, and it doesn't automatically mean that we're right and you're wrong. At this stage, all we ask is that you continue to read as we begin to explain things in a bit more detail. By the end of the book, you may still not agree with everything we're saying – and that's fine. However, it's not our intention to waste your time, and when we suggest you continue reading, it's because we feel confident that you'll still be able to find at least some ideas and suggestions that could be helpful for you and your voices to develop a more peaceful relationship. In the meantime, if it's too hard to consider being compassionate to the voices themselves, then perhaps you can try focusing on building compassion for the experience of voice-hearing more broadly – as well as for yourself as a voice-hearer.

Understandings that can reduce shame and build confidence

In CFT, we aim to develop understandings of ourselves and our experiences that make us feel less shame while also helping us to feel more empowered and confident. In particular, we consider the way our brains have evolved over time to help us recognise that they are actually really tricky, and that it's not our fault. In Chapter 2, we described some of the things that our brains naturally do – things that make complete sense in the context of many millions of years of human evolution, but which cause us real problems today. We described how our brains: 1) pay more attention to threats; 2) create loops; and 3) get shaped by our motives and emotions (which we focused on using the three "multiple selves" of angry, anxious, and sad).

Understanding our brains and experiences as a result of evolution can reduce shame by helping us to realise that the way we react to negative events is not our fault. However, while the "it's not your fault" message is very helpful for making us feel less ashamed, it's not enough on its own to support compassionate engagement and action. For example, in the medical model of voice-hearing (described earlier), there is also a clear "it's not your fault" message (i.e. it's not your fault because the voices are caused by your illness). So this can also be experienced as removing blame and shame. However, explaining our experiences as the result of a disease (that is out of our control) can leave us feeling helpless and dependent on solutions that we do not have much power over, such as psychiatric drugs prescribed by mental health professionals. Of course, both these things can also be very helpful. However, the problem is that they may create "out-of-control" feelings that lead to anxiety (such as worries about psychosis, or about relapse) as well as feelings of helplessness that can lead to depression (for example, "there is nothing I can do about my illness because my mental health workers know more about my experiences than I do"). Interestingly, a recent review of research studies found that ways of understanding psychosis which are based on disease can actually *increase* stigma for people with these experiences [42]. This chapter suggests that an "*it's not your fault, but it is your responsibility*" message is an important first step in compassionate engagement and action: "It's not your fault" helps reduce our sense of shame; however, "It is your responsibility" is empowering because it reminds us that there are a lot of choices you can make in reshaping, transforming, and improving your ability to cope with your experiences.

The resource box illustrates this by describing the experiences of a voice-hearer called Emily. After listening to her family and healthcare workers, Emily had developed an understanding about her voices that was based on the medical model. She saw her voices as being "symptoms" of an illness which were best left to professionals to deal with. Although she didn't blame herself or anyone else for her voices, this understanding did leave her feeling disempowered and dependent on medication (most likely, for the rest of her life). This understanding also played into Emily's long-standing concerns about feeling different to other people, and the worries she has always had that being different also made her a target for other people's negative judgements, rejection, and harm.

RESOURCE BOX

EXAMPLE: Emily

Emily is a 27-year-old woman who finds it hard to leave the house because she believes that people in the street are talking about her and laughing at her. She hears voices of groups of people talking among themselves, saying words like "weirdo" and "mad" in reference to her. Emily finds this very distressing. She has been told by her family and mental health services that this is not real and "just part of her illness", and that she has to take antipsychotics to treat the chemical imbalance caused by schizophrenia, which is making her hear and believe things which aren't real. Medication has not got rid of Emily's voices and she is concerned about its side effects, particularly weight gain and how tired it makes her feel. However, she is afraid to stop taking it because she has been told that without it, she will end up in hospital. Emily also worries that people might be laughing at her because they know about her schizophrenia diagnosis and that she is a "mad" person.

Earlier in her life, Emily was bullied by a group of girls at school, who spread rumours about her and called her names. This made Emily feel excluded from the whole year group because she had no idea who had heard these rumours or not. Maybe everyone knew and was laughing at her? One day when she was 14, the girls followed her into a tunnel, where they pushed her around and grabbed her bag, while laughing and recording it on their phones. It's a blurry memory for Emily and she never told anyone – partly because she felt embarrassed, and partly because she was afraid it might make the bullying worse.

Emily's experience	Moving towards an understanding that brings in ideas from CFT
Voice-hearing experience I can hear people talking about me every time I go out. They are laughing at me and saying that I'm weird. *Social experience* Everyone tells me this is part of my schizophrenia. They say I've got a mental illness that is caused by something that has gone wrong in my brain. This makes me feel different to everyone else, like I have a brain that is broken or faulty. And I need to take drugs to fix my brain. I am mad, different, and everyone can see that.	My brain isn't broken, it has been doing its job of threat-protection very well, under extremely difficult circumstances. Scanning for real and potential threats was *very useful* under the circumstances of being bullied and excluded at school. There is nothing to fix in my brain, it's more a question of reorganising and growing. It's *not my fault* that our human brains are tricky. They have evolved in this way, with built-in 'better safe than sorry' patterns. It's also *not my fault* that my early social experiences have shaped how my threat system has become more active over time. I had to use my threat system a lot at school, so it has been well exercised and is easily switched on. It's a bit like training up a muscle in the gym; the more we exercise a muscle, the stronger it becomes.

This example shows how developing an understanding that was empowering and reduced her sense of shame was helpful for Emily to start thinking about herself and her voices in a different way. It opened a path for her and her future that was less dependent on professionals and medications, and which gave her more choices and control over what she wanted to address from her past (like painful memories and emotions), and what she wanted to shape and grow moving forward (such as her emotional responses and social experiences). By understanding her voice-hearing in the context of fears and difficulties in her life, Emily's focus shifted towards how she might be able to resolve these threat-based events. We will come back to Emily later in this chapter and see how her understanding about her experiences generally – and voices in particular – developed over time. For now, we would like to talk about an approach to understanding voices that considers their possible *function* in our lives.

What job or function might voices be performing for us?

Protecting us from future harm (from others)

In Chapter 2, we described how, for many people, the relationship they have with their voices can involve roles that they also experience in their social lives. As you may remember, CFT pays close attention to two particular types of social relationships: those that are dominant (which make us feel threatened) and those that are subordinate (which make us feel powerless) [14]. As such, the experience of taking a subordinate role in relation to a powerful voice may be very similar to roles we have taken in real life with people who have had power over us, especially if we have been a victim of trauma. In other words, the voice can create the same response *in us* that we've used in the past to protect ourselves from harm. Framed in this way, the voice-hearing experience itself could be considered *helpful* (or at least functional, in the sense that it is performing an important psychological job for us).

At this point, it might feel rather nonsensical to describe voices as "helpful" when they can cause so much distress in our lives, so please allow us to explain what we mean. When we say that voices are performing a job for us, what we mean is that their presence is protecting us from future harm by switching on our threat system and prompting a particular response in us that has helped to protect us in the past. To understand this a bit more, it is helpful to think of how, after a stressful life event, it is protective to have our threat detection and responses "switched on" to prevent further harm. Again, this may seem like a contradiction, because these responses in themselves (such as feeling very paranoid or not wanting to be around people) can cause further distress. Remember, however, that *our tricky brains aren't concerned with whether we're happy or not – their main focus is only on keeping us safe*. Now that we understand this (and, importantly, understand that this response is not our fault), we can see how a voice's purpose may be "helpful" when it makes us feel like we want to "stay on guard", "keep a distance from others", or "lock the doors and windows". It doesn't necessarily matter what the actual *content* of the voice is; the important thing, as far as threat-protection and survival is concerned, are the mental, physical, and behavioural responses that the voice creates *in us*. Exploring this process is the beginning of developing our compassionate engagement with our experiences. And then, when we are ready, we can use our new knowledge to help us choose the right compassionate action.

CHECK-IN BOX

TRIGGER WARNING

In this section, we will be using examples of distressing life events to illustrate how voices might be linked to threat-protection processes. One of the examples involves childhood sexual abuse, and another involves physical violence. These are very upsetting topics, and it's understandable that reading about these things can create reactions in people. If you think that either of these topics might trigger a strong emotional response in you, then please just take a moment before reading on to think about how you might take care of yourself. Is there a grounding practice that helps you? Are you able to use some of the ideas we shared in Chapter 3 about creating safeness?

Remember that strong emotions do eventually pass. What usually happens is that they peak, and then gradually settle again over time. Your Compassionate Self is there to guide you through the peak – a bit like a surfer riding a wave that starts off big, and then gradually gets smaller as the surfer approaches the shore.

An example of this process at work could be with someone who has been sexually abused in childhood, and then, as an adult, hears a voice that says: "you asked for it; you deserved everything that happened to you". The content of the voice does not necessarily have to match the content of the trauma, and the source of threat doesn't necessarily have to match it either (so, for example, the voice may or may not sound like the person who carried out the real-life abuse). However, the protective response produced by the voice is still likely to be very relevant for protecting against the harm associated with sexual abuse. For example, some responses we could have to such a voice might include:

- Feeling depressed and not wanting to be around people
- Believing that we don't deserve to ever have enjoyable sex and relationships
- Not taking care of our bodies or physical appearance
- Avoiding getting too close to people

Some of these responses could be protective in that they reduce the likelihood of sexual encounters from happening in the first place. Other responses could be protective in that they reduce the level of harm caused in future sexual encounters. For example, seeing yourself as worthless and not caring about your body is potentially protective against the level of emotional pain and trauma that could occur with future abuse. So, while the *solution* (for example, avoiding other people and feeling lonely) is distressing, we may feel that it is still better than the *problem* it is attempting to prevent (being hurt even more in the future).

At this point, it might be helpful to remember what we were saying before (in Chapter 2) about our threat system being like a smoke detector that is programmed to be "better safe than sorry". In the same way that the smoke alarm gets easily activated to protect us from fires (even when we've only burnt the toast), our threat system is easily activated to protect us from future harm (even when we are hearing a voice, and no one is physically around to harm us).

Protecting us from our own difficult feelings and memories

The role of voices in protecting us may not only apply to potential outside threats (from other people) but also to *internal* threats (from our own feared emotions, memories, and mental states). An example of an internal threat that is relevant to survivors of very stressful events may be the fear of one's own feelings of helplessness and powerlessness. In this case, it may be that the voice's role is to keep our mind focused on a current threat in the outside world, because the alternative – confronting our own internal states and memories of helplessness and powerlessness – may be far harder. For example, voices are very effective at attention-grabbing and keeping the threat system focused in a particular direction (towards the voice). Here, the voice is keeping us in "fight" and "flight" mode, which may feel safer than being in more defeat-type states like "freeze" and "submit". Again, the important aspect is not necessarily the *content* of the voice, but more the process of what the voice is doing for us.

In other situations, the voice might be helping someone to avoid an emotion that is particularly difficult for them, such as anger. For instance, it might have been very useful for someone to hide their anger (or their angry self) during an overwhelming experience because that emotion may have made the situation a lot worse. Consider the example of Tom, who grew up with an aggressive father. As a 4-year-old boy, it was far safer for Tom not to show his real feelings because it would have been very dangerous for him to get angry towards his dad. This meant that Tom grew up to fear not only his dad, but also his own anger, and this was a pattern that continued throughout school. He became very good at learning to bury his anger and avoid conflict; and, if conflict was unavoidable, he learnt that it felt safer to back down as quickly as possible. However, later in life, Tom began to hear angry voices that said things like: "You're pathetic" and "I'm going to make you pay for being such a loser". In the moment of hearing those voices, where is Tom's attention? What emotion is he feeling? What is his response? The attention is probably towards the voice (the threat); the emotion is probably fear; and the response is probably to feel beaten down and wanting to escape. What he is **not** feeling is anger. In a sense, the voice is "holding" his anger, rather than Tom himself. The anger that he might otherwise rightly have towards his father has unfortunately become something that feels dangerous for him, so it remains contained within the voices and redirected towards himself – a safer target for it. This process is often referred to as "dissociation" and is a very common human response to threat, stress, and trauma.

CHECK-IN BOX

How does that feel for you? This idea that our voices may (at some level) be helping us, or trying to help us? You might think that sounds ridiculous at first, because much of your experience with voices may be the opposite to that. For many, their voices can feel *anything but* helpful. Of course, we know how distressing voice-hearing can be, and how devastating the impact of voices can be on people's lives. So, if you experience your own voices as *unhelpful* that is completely understandable and would make perfect sense to us. In fact, this is such a common contradiction that Marius Romme and Sandra Escher, the co-founders of the Hearing Voices Movement, even had a phrase for it. They said that voices are both the "problem" and the "solution".

In this section, we are inviting you to take a moment to consider your voices in a slightly different way: instead of focusing on the voices themselves, or the words they are saying, try for a minute to focus on the *response created in you* when you hear the voices. Noticing this *response in you* might be something that helps you to link your experience of voice-hearing to other experiences in your life. And this could be a path towards developing new understandings and ideas about the role of your voices.

Some of the most distressing voice-hearing experiences can be when people hear the voice of someone they know, or have known, who has hurt them in real life. And what's even more distressing is when they believe that the voice they're hearing is actually coming from the abuser themselves (which, of course, is understandable given that it sounds like the same voice). Again, with this type of voice, instead of focusing on where it's coming from, we might just invite the person to consider the *response created in them* when they hear the voice. And to ask the question why, if they have been abused in the past, might it be protective for voice-hearing to keep creating this response in the days/months/years after the abuse?

Drawing our attention to past distress and memories of threat that have not yet been resolved

So far in this chapter, we have been focusing on voices that tend to relate to us in a particular way. The "purpose" of these voices very much lies in the relationships and roles they create, both for themselves (e.g. dominant) and for us (e.g. subordinate). Often these voices are experienced as having a mind of their own; for example, they may have a distinct personality, hold a particular opinion, and show a changing awareness of what's happening around them. It is very similar to a person-to-person relationship, in that these voices are able to engage and react to conversations as they carry out their roles. However, we will now turn our attention to another type of voice that cannot hold conversations, and that tends to just repeat the same things over and over. This is less like a relationship with another person, but more like a recorded message being played back to us. In our CFT workshops, we have usually referred to these as "tape recorder" voices. These voices can take different forms, but their main feature is that they replay a message that's linked to a memory of something that's happened in the past. They are similar to flashbacks, in that they are often re-running some piece of information from a memory, such as the voice of a critical parent or an abuser. Often, it is not only the memory about the *source* of threat (for example, the sound/tone of the other person's voice may be different) but rather the whole scene, including the memory of our own *response* (for example, our feelings of fear or anger, along with our bodily urges to escape or to fight back).

When thinking about the purpose of these memory-based voices, we might want to ask ourselves "why is my voice replaying this memory to me?" In fact, there are two slightly different ways of approaching this question, one which focuses on the memory itself ("by replaying this memory to me, what is my voice drawing my attention to, and why?") and another which focuses on the emotional and bodily response that are triggered ("by replaying this memory to me, what response is my voice creating in me, and why?").

In the trauma field, doctors and researchers have often asked a similar question about why people experience flashbacks: "by replaying flashbacks of a trauma memory, what are our brains trying to do?" There are a number of theories about this. For example, some people suggest that our brains may be making attempts to process the distressing event (sometimes called the "completion principle", in the sense our brain wants to make a whole picture of what happened [43]). Others have suggested that our brains may be attempting to re-live and master the negative emotions; in other words, learning to tolerate the feelings associated with what happened to us. In both cases, we can understand why this would be helpful. On the one hand, it would be helpful to have a "complete" (integrated) memory of what has happened so that we can better protect ourselves in the future. However, it would also be helpful to have the ability to tolerate the strong emotions, so that we are not so overwhelmed if they happen again. Could there be a similar process with memory-based voices? Could it be that these voices are drawing our attention to some threat-based memory that we have not yet integrated? Or to some threat-based feelings that we have not yet learnt how to tolerate?

In the resource box, we have created a table that lists some examples of the different types of voices that we have come across, along with some examples of their possible roles/functions. This was inspired by a similar table in an article co-authored by one of us (Eleanor) with two colleagues in 2017 [44]. Our table includes a distinction between the two main types of voices that we have mentioned in this chapter; those which can think, respond, converse, and seem to have a mind of their own, and those which are more linked to memories that replay the same message "on repeat". This is not supposed to be a complete list of all voices; in fact, far from it – we know how hugely varied people's voice-hearing experiences are. This list is more to help get us thinking about different voices, what kinds of relationship we have with them, and to grow our curiosity about their possible function in our lives.

RESOURCE BOX

Types, relationship styles, and functions of voices

Type	Relationship style with voice-hearer	Possible function
Voices with a mind and opinion of their own	**Suspicious voices** "danger" "don't trust her" "he's going to hurt you"	Protecting me from further harm by scanning for threats and potential dangers
	Threatening/abusive voices "I'm going to hurt you/ punish you/kill you"	Protecting me from further harm by: 1) creating an internal guide of what a dangerous person is like 2) creating a (powerful) protective response in me that can match the (extreme) level of potential harm from another person
	Blaming /shaming voices "it's your fault" "you deserved it"	Protecting me from unbearable feelings of helplessness and defeat by providing me with a sense of control and choice (i.e. a sense that there is something I can actually do about this to avoid further harm)
	Commanding voices "do this job the way I tell you" "you should always listen to my advice"	Protecting me from overwhelming feelings and memories by focusing my attention on rules and tasks. This gives me a sense of control that I can do something to stay safe – that I can avoid harm through specific actions
	Voices that create responses that are: – **Submissive** – **Compliant** – **Appeasing** "always put your friends' needs before your own" "don't ever contradict your boss"	Protecting me from further harm by: – Feeling withdrawn and undeserving of other people's attention – Keeping my head down – Avoiding conflict/ confrontation – Keeping others happy

Voices linked to memories	Can be any of the above but more like a tape recorder on repeat	Drawing my attention to a threat-based memory from the past that has not yet been processed. My mind is still trying to make sense of it, because the memory is stored in a fragmented way, and needs to be resolved as a "complete" (integrated) memory so I can better protect myself in the future (such as being able to predict and respond to threats).

Do your voices fit into any of these descriptions?

This is not a complete list, but just a list of some of the common ones that we hear about and come across. We know there are lots of other types. Some voices may also have more than one role. For example, it may be both commanding and suspicious at the same time.

If you do have a voice that fits any these descriptions, could there be a similar 'possible function' going on to the one we've suggested? Remember these are just examples to get us thinking about voices in this way. Don't worry if you feel that none of them fit your experiences.

Some examples of people making sense of their voices

In this final section of the chapter, we will be bringing these ideas together about understanding the function of voices by using some examples of people's stories. You already met Emily earlier, and in this section, you will meet three more voice-hearers: Alan, Deepa, and Kwame. We will describe their personal stories and experiences, and we will map out the possible functions of their voices using a three-column diagram which covers 1) early experiences, 2) key threats, and 3) possible functions for the voice(s). Finally, you will be invited to map out a similar diagram for yourself.

Alan

Alan is a 54-year-old man who communicates with the voices of spirits. Alan feels that this ability, and his access to the spiritual world, gives him useful insights and knowledge about people's hidden (*real*) intentions. However, it also makes him a target for evil spirits who want to take his abilities away from him. These evil spirits make threats like "we're going to kill you". Alan's mother died when he was very young, but his father never talked about her death and avoided Alan's questions with responses like, "she was unwell" and "it's probably better if you don't know". Alan's voices started when he was 22, around the time that he discovered his father had cheated on his mother with another woman at the time of Alan's birth. The spirit voices were initially useful, offering guidance and advice. However, five years later, after the breakup of a long term relationship, some voices started to become more threatening.

Alan wanted to look back on his life to try to understand his voices in the context of his difficult experiences. The following map that he created has three columns, describing how his voice-hearing experiences may have a specific purpose in relation to some of his key fears/threats (both external and internal). Although the voices had an initial role in providing companionship and guidance, Alan recognised that there had always been a "suspicious" theme in his voices, in that they were often trying to work out people's hidden intentions. Alan also realised that he had never grieved the loss of his mother; partly because he didn't feel safe with sad emotions, and partly because her death was something that wasn't talked about, so there was never an opportunity.

Alan's map:

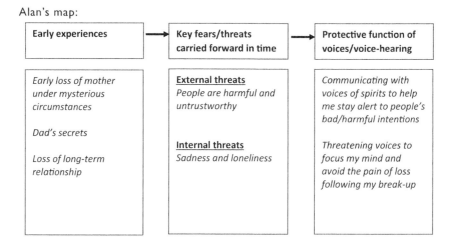

Early experiences	Key fears/threats carried forward in time	Protective function of voices/voice-hearing
Early loss of mother under mysterious circumstances *Dad's secrets* *Loss of long-term relationship*	**External threats** *People are harmful and untrustworthy* **Internal threats** *Sadness and loneliness*	*Communicating with voices of spirits to help me stay alert to people's bad/harmful intentions* *Threatening voices to focus my mind and avoid the pain of loss following my break-up*

Deepa

Deepa is a 32-year-old woman who hears the voices of her neighbours making negative remarks about her and planning to attack her. Deepa grew up in a care home after her mother gave her up for adoption. At the age of 19, Deepa married and had a daughter. She had always felt that her employers treated her differently to her white co-workers, and ten years ago she got into a fight at work after a long period of being racially harassed and taunted by colleagues. She was badly injured in the fight, but because she was blamed for starting it, she ended up losing her job. Deepa became very depressed, and occasionally lost her temper with her husband, sometimes screaming and smashing plates. Her husband started to become scared of her unpredictable mood and grew concerned about the safety of their daughter. The marriage broke down and her husband took their daughter away to live abroad. Shortly afterwards, he broke off all contact with Deepa. Deepa blames herself for losing her job and her family.

Deepa mapped out some of her key fears and threats that had resulted from her difficult life experiences and memories. She developed an understanding of her voices as being linked to her experiences of racism and discrimination, in the sense that these socially threatening experiences had required her threat system to be highly active. One of the functions of her voices is to keep her *threat detection* switched on (by scanning for threats from potential racism such as from the house next door) and to keep her *threat responses* switched on (keeping safe by avoiding people, keeping her head down, and avoiding anger and conflict).

Deepa's map:

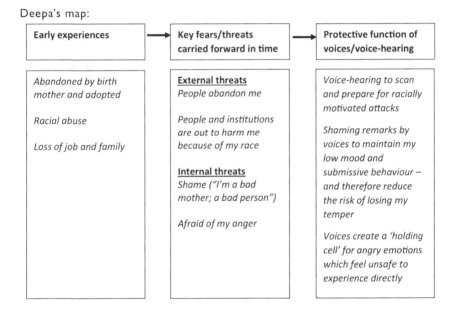

Early experiences	Key fears/threats carried forward in time	Protective function of voices/voice-hearing
Abandoned by birth mother and adopted *Racial abuse* *Loss of job and family*	**External threats** *People abandon me* *People and institutions are out to harm me because of my race* **Internal threats** *Shame ("I'm a bad mother; a bad person")* *Afraid of my anger*	*Voice-hearing to scan and prepare for racially motivated attacks* *Shaming remarks by voices to maintain my low mood and submissive behaviour – and therefore reduce the risk of losing my temper* *Voices create a 'holding cell' for angry emotions which feel unsafe to experience directly*

Kwame

Kwame is a 40-year-old man who, between the ages of 10 and 14, was repeatedly sexually assaulted. He hears hostile memory-based voices that say things like, "sit on my knee" and other shaming voices that make comments like "you're dirty", "you deserved it", and "you enjoyed it". For most of his adult life, Kwame has fought with his voices and tried to get rid of them, but he has recently explored a new meaning that they might be understandable and meaningful responses to extremely distressing life events. The following map that Kwame created considers the protective role of his voices; for example, the blaming and shaming voices provide him with an illusion of control: "if I'm a bad person, then I hold responsibility and control over what has happened. That means there is something I can do about it, and I can control/influence the future by being a better person". He could see how his memory-based voices were directly linked to distressing events in his life. He therefore began to consider them as helpful communicators, signals, or signposts towards unresolved issues from the past that needed his compassionate attention and care. Kwame had also felt great guilt and shame at experiencing physical pleasure during his abuse, so another important thing he learned was that human bodies automatically react to sexual stimulation in ways that are beyond the mind's control. By realising that his physical response did not mean that he had "enjoyed" what happened to him, Kwame was able to direct compassion to those parts of himself that had felt so confused and betrayed.

Kwame's map:

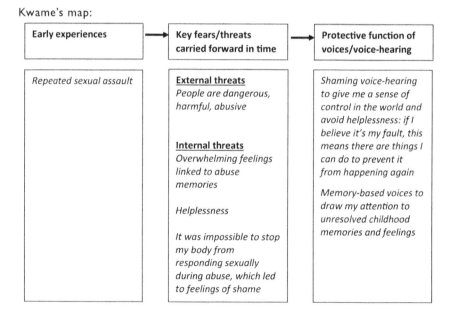

Early experiences	Key fears/threats carried forward in time	Protective function of voices/voice-hearing
Repeated sexual assault	**External threats** *People are dangerous, harmful, abusive* **Internal threats** *Overwhelming feelings linked to abuse memories* *Helplessness* *It was impossible to stop my body from responding sexually during abuse, which led to feelings of shame*	*Shaming voice-hearing to give me a sense of control in the world and avoid helplessness: if I believe it's my fault, this means there are things I can do to prevent it from happening again* *Memory-based voices to draw my attention to unresolved childhood memories and feelings*

Emily

Emily is the 27-year-old woman who we met earlier in the chapter. As a quick reminder, the voices she hears are of people talking among themselves in groups, saying "weirdo" and "mad", and laughing at her. As described earlier, Emily's school days were really tough, with constant bullying, rumour-spreading, and a terrifying experience in a tunnel where she was intimidated and humiliated by a group of other girls. When Emily started mapping out the threat-protective function of her voice-hearing experiences, she noticed a clear link between how the voices make her feel and behave *now* (in the present) and how the school bullies used to make her feel and behave *then* (in the past). She therefore wondered if her voices had started as a way of protecting her from similar sorts of dangers. Her voices are scanning for the threat of this happening again, making her particularly cautious of people in groups. Specifically, the voices are paying close attention to any words or phrases that might signal threat. This is why she is terrified of the psychiatric diagnosis, as it could be another label that makes her a target. The voices are also creating a number of responses in her, such as feeling different to others, not fitting in, and keeping a distance from people. Although these responses are distressing, their purpose is still to protect Emily by helping her to keep safe and avoid future harm. In terms of the threat system – which operates by the principle of "better safe than sorry" – these are very understandable responses.

Emily's map:

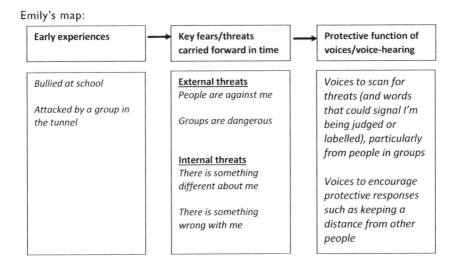

You

If you feel ready, we'd now like to invite you to think about developing a compassionate understanding of your own voices. In the practical box, we have laid this out as a step-by-step exercise for you to walk through, starting with some questions to consider, then a completed map to remind you of some of the themes that go into each box, followed by a blank map for you to fill in your own boxes. You may need to spend some time thinking about this; for example, not everyone has a clear memory of difficult things that have happened to them because the protective process of dissociation (described earlier) causes us to block them out. Or maybe you feel you haven't gone through an "extreme" life event like the examples of abuse, loss, and bullying we gave here. If so, then remember that human pain is relative, and everyone experiences negative events in different ways. Please don't feel that a distressing event in your life is too "minor" to count. Some of us feel things very deeply that others would not be concerned by, and vice versa. This is very common, and not our fault. It's just part of being human with these tricky brains of ours.

Remember too that this is entirely optional. Only do this if you feel comfortable; if you like, you can always ask another person to walk through this with you. We understand that this is a difficult exercise, potentially bringing you into contact with difficult memories and feelings. And this is hard. Like we've been saying all the way through this book, compassion is hard.

Compassion is the courage to descend into the reality of human experience.
– Paul Gilbert

The process of developing compassionate understandings and responses to ourselves can involve shining a light into the most difficult parts of our experience, including the parts that we fear or dislike the most. This takes time and there is no rush. You are entirely in control here – so please take care of yourself.

PRACTICAL BOX

EXERCISE: Exploring your voices and their possible function

To start with, here are some general questions for you to consider:

- When you hear voices, what responses do you think are created in you?
- Do these responses remind you of any other relationships in your life?
- Is there any reason why your threat-response system might be switching on?
- What might your voices be protecting or distracting you from?
- Is there an emotion, a memory, or a part that you might be avoiding?

We're now going to try and map this out in a diagram, using three columns: 1) early experiences, 2) key fears/threats, 3) protective function. The first one is filled in as an illustration, and then the second one is left blank for you to complete with your own experiences. (It might be helpful to refer back to the table on page 116 for more examples of possible functions.)

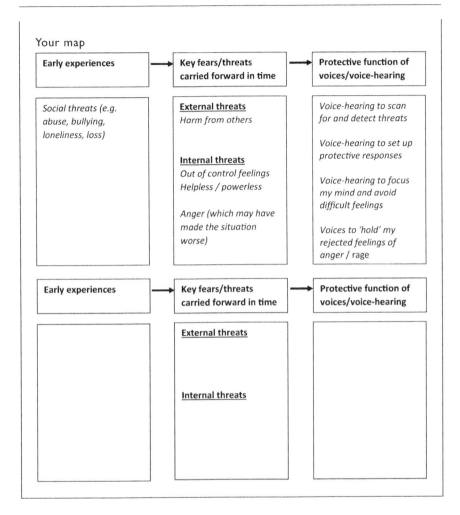

Thank you for staying with us this far during the book. We realise we have probably introduced several ideas and suggestions that were unfamiliar to you – some of which might have felt uncomfortable or threatening – and we respect your courage and appreciate your patience for being prepared to listen to what we have to say. Whenever you're ready, we look forward to discussing these ideas with you further in the next chapter. However, in the meantime, thank you again to you and your voices for taking this journey with us.

Chapter 7

Developing a compassionate relationship with your voices

Chapter summary

How can we put our Compassionate Self to work in relating to voices?

This chapter brings together all the ideas we've discussed so far to address an important question: what can help us switch from relationships with our voices that are based in threat towards those which are more caring and compassionate? There are various practices we can use to help this shift which will be described in detail, and which you'll also have a chance to try out for yourself:

- Role-play and acting/embodiment techniques
- Imagery
- Letter-writing

We will then come back to our four voice-hearers – Alan, Deepa, Kwame, and Emily – to discover how their Compassionate Self relates to their voices. Where a voice has an identified job or function, we will see how the Compassionate Self might try to help specifically with what's *behind* that voice. However, where a voice does not have an identified job or function, we will learn some more general ways that the Compassionate Self might relate and respond to voices.

Introduction

The previous chapter focused on developing an understanding of voices, and the role they may play in your life, which can help reduce the sense of conflict and struggle you may sometimes feel toward them. Moving away from these kinds of hostile, argumentative relationships with voices is a crucial part of CFT, because of the way they are linked to our threat system – which, in turn, activates threat-based emotions and responses.

In CFT, we are mainly concerned with ways of understanding and approaching our experiences that move us away from threat-based mindsets centred on conflict and competition, and towards ways of thinking and being which are more co-operative and caring. Our brains have the built-in hardwiring for both types

DOI: 10.4324/9781003166269-10

of mindsets: one which is focused on protecting us from social threats, and one which is more focused on social caring. This chapter will now turn to focus on the kinds of responses and actions we can take towards developing a more peaceful, collaborative, and compassionate relationship with voices.

We will continue to follow the stories of our four voice-hearers (Emily, Alan, Deepa, and Kwame) to see how their understandings of voices (Chapter 6) influence their compassionate responses and actions (this chapter). We will also describe some more general examples of responding and relating to voices, even if there is no clear understanding of their role. So, although an understanding can be very useful for some people, it is not essential. Hopefully this chapter will still offer some helpful ideas, even if you haven't developed your own map in Chapter 6.

The courage of compassionate relating to voices

"Hello."

"What do you want loser?"

"I want to understand you. I want to help you feel safe."

"Safe? Nothing's safe around here. If it wasn't for me you'd be . . ."

"I know you're trying to help me. Thank you. Thank you for reminding me that I get scared. You're right, I do. But I want to start overcoming my fears now. I'm ready."

"You want to get rid of me."

"No I don't. I don't want to get rid of anyone. We can work on this together."

– Quote from *"Compassion for Voices"* film [29]

In 2015, we made a short animated film called *"Compassion for Voices: a tale of courage and hope"* [29]. One of us (Charlie) did the writing and directing with an animator, Kate Anderson, and the other (Eleanor) added some suggestions to the script and then did the narration and voiceover with another colleague, Rufus May.

There is a key message in this film which shows an important shift in how we might relate to voices: away from seeing them as *enemies*, and towards seeing them as having a role as *allies* (for example, playing a part in understanding and resolving our emotional concerns). In the previous quote, there is a clear intention of wanting to work together with a voice and collaborate towards a shared goal (*"I don't want to get rid of anyone. We can work on this together"*).

This shift from conflict to collaboration can be challenging. However, as we have seen in the earlier chapters of this book, this is very much a challenge that we can train and prepare for. There is preparation we can do in our bodies, in our minds, and in our relationships. As we feel safer, more grounded, and more connected to the people around us, we will become better prepared for the challenge of relating to our voices in a compassionate way. It's a bit like a runner who does training and preparation before running a marathon. Do they just turn up on the start line, expecting to be ready to run 26 miles? Of course not; they do months of training beforehand, getting themselves ready for the task ahead. In the *Compassion for Voices* film, it's similar for Stuart, who does a lot of training for his Compassionate Self to help get it prepared for the courage of relating to his voices.

In the film (please see the practical box for a webpage), Stuart is shown practicing exercises with his body posture, acting/embodiment techniques, breathing rhythm, facial expression, and imagery. He keeps practicing these exercises regularly at home, sometimes standing in front of the bedroom mirror. The film also shows that this isn't a short training period – it doesn't happen overnight. In fact, we see Stuart flipping through the months of his wall calendar, and we see the tree outside losing its leaves as the seasons change. Preparing our body and mind for compassionate relating takes time. This is no surprise – remember, compassion is all about moving towards the most distressing parts of our experience. This is hard. You could say that it's a bit like the emotional equivalent of running a marathon. However, please don't feel discouraged by this. In our opinion, the time taken is a positive thing, because it helps the changes we make to become more deep-seated and lasting. It also means that they occur at a gentle, manageable pace, as the new habits we learn become a natural part of our routine. For example, think about the idea of a "crash diet". It's well known that losing a lot of weight very quickly is stressful for the body and often makes it difficult to keep off the weight we lose. However, losing it slowly over time through manageable changes can make the results much more permanent. It stops being a diet and instead just becomes part of our lifestyle.

A number of people have found the *Compassion for Voices* film helpful in guiding them through the process of improving the relationship with their voices. We have therefore developed an exercise in the practical box which will take you through the video, step by step, and ask you some questions about how this film might relate to your own experience.

PRACTICAL BOX

VIDEO: Compassion for Voices: a tale of courage and hope

You can find the *"Compassion for Voices"* video on YouTube and on the webpage: www.relatingtovoices.com/videos

In this video, we see Stuart going through his daily life. As he moves through his routine, the symbols on his chest show how his emotion systems (the "three circles" from Chapter 1) are balanced. Importantly, we can see how the balance of Stuart's emotions are linked to his experiences with voices, as well as what is happening in his social environments.

EXERCISE: Are any of Stuart's experiences relevant to your own?

We will now invite you to watch this video again, but this time going through it a bit more slowly, pressing pause at certain time points so that you can answer some questions. The time points and the corresponding questions are shown in this table.

Scene	Time	Questions
1. Stuart's threat system kicks in	0:30	*When do you notice your threat system kicking in?* . . . . *How does this link to your environment and social experiences?* . . . . *How does this link to your voices?* . . . .
2. Stuart meets his therapist	1:46	*If you have ever met a mental health professional, how did that feel to you at first?* . . . . *What did your voices say about meeting them?* . . . . *What do they say now?* . . . .
3. Stuart's Compassionate Self develops over time . . . using practices in: a) Soothing breathing	3:38	It takes Stuart time to develop his Compassionate Self and requires plenty of practice and encouragement. *When is the best time for you to practice? (e.g. mornings or evenings?)* . . . . *Do you find it useful to give yourself reminders? (e.g. on your phone or with notes in your home?)* . . . . Stuart uses a range of strategies to activate his soothing system and to create cues of safeness.

Scene	Time	Questions
b) Imagery		Which strategies do you find easiest?
		....
		Which strategies do you find hardest?
		....
c) Face, tone, and		How would your Compassionate Self help you with the bits you find hard? What would s/he say?
		....
4. Compassionate relating to his voices	2:59	If it felt safe enough, is there anything you would like to ask your voices?
		....
		What would be difficult about talking to them?
		....
		What qualities would you need to draw on to talk to your voices? (e.g. courage and wisdom)
		....
5. Feeling safe in relation to his voices	4:21	What helps you to stay calm and grounded when your voices are there?
		....
		If you were to pack a kitbag of things that made you feel safe, what would you put in it? (e.g. the safety and safeness kit in Chapter 3)
		....
6. Part of the family, but not running the show	4:29	How would you build bridges with your voice(s)?
		....
		If you thought of your voice(s) as being different members of your team with different roles, what specific role would each team member have? Voice. . . . . Role. . . . . Voice. . . . . Role. . . . .

Images reproduced with permission from the *Compassion for Voices* production collaboration (C. Heriot-Maitland and K. Anderson).

How did you get on? Has this film encouraged you to think about or do anything differently? Is there someone else you know who you might benefit from watching this film?

Mapping out voices and relationships with voices

Creating visual maps can be a useful exercise for helping to represent the different relationships we have with our voices. To begin with, we can represent their characteristics using different sizes, shapes, distances, and colours (for example, if I have a powerful, intrusive voice, I might draw this on the map as a large shape that's positioned very close to me). These maps can also be a helpful starting point for making "profiles" of each voice. For example, once we've mapped out all of the voices and their various positions in relation to ourselves, we can start to think a bit more about them, such as whether they have a name, an age, and what they sound like. We can also think about their specific motives and intentions, as well as their fears and concerns. For example, what problems or issues does the voice seem most focused on? Is the voice trying to help in some way? When did this voice come into your life? When is this voice most active? What does this voice "do" for you? In a study of 100 voice-hearers that one of us (Eleanor) carried out, it was found that 78% of people could be supported to identify "who/what do the voices represent", and 94% of voice-hearers could identify "what problems do the voices represent" [45]. If you are interested, there is an excellent tool designed specifically for profiling voices called the *Maastricht Interview* [46].

In Chapter 5, we used the example of John in an exercise for mapping out your multiple selves (angry, anxious, and sad). We will now invite you to do a similar exercise that extends this map to include your voices. In the next practical box, we start off with the multiple selves from Chapter 5 (please see diagram A) and then we add in voices (diagram B). You can use the empty box to map out your own personal version of diagram B. In our example, we have shown that a "hostile voice" is quite close to us and slightly to the left. This voice doesn't have a name, but we've referred to it with a description of what role it takes (*hostile*) in relation to us.

We have also shown in diagram B that there are two other parts *behind* this voice (further out to the left): a "traumatised part", and a "helpless part". This is a way of representing that the hostile voice may be protecting these parts. This was discussed in Chapter 6, where we explored the possible functions of voices, and considered how some of them may be protective against *internal threats*, such as trauma memories and other unbearable feelings. The map in diagram B is a way of illustrating this.

PRACTICAL BOX

EXERCISE: Mapping relationships between parts

Mapping exercises can help to develop different ways of relating to voices, away from threat-protection and towards empathy and curiosity. From a CFT perspective, this marks the beginning of the shift towards relating to voices more compassionately. The first four boxes have a series of maps (A to D) to show how a voice-hearer's relationship with voices might change over time as their Compassionate Self comes in to organise these relationships. After this is a blank box for you to have a go at mapping out your own voices.

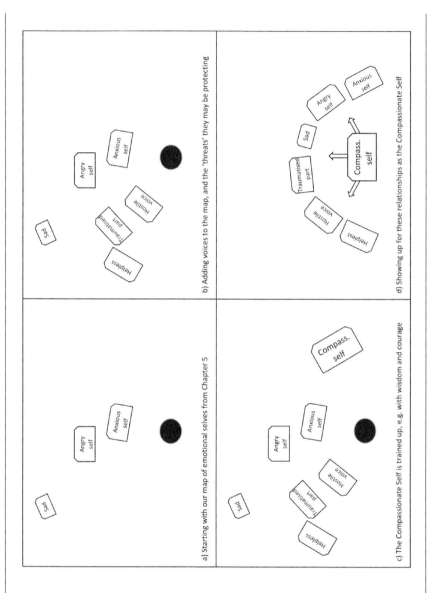

Diagram adapted with permission from Heriot-Maitland, C. (2022) in G. Simos & P. Gilbert (Eds.) Compassion Focused Therapy in Clinical Practice. Routledge [39]

You can use this space to draw your own map:

Mapping what is *behind* the voice can also be very important to prepare us for what may start to emerge if the relationship with voices begins to change. For example, if an angry voice starts to speak in a more calm and supportive way, it may be that other feelings and memories that were *behind* the voice could start to surface. It would be helpful if the Compassionate Self was ready to encounter this, if and when it happens.

In the CFT approach to voice-hearing, we often use one of Paul Gilbert's metaphors – the Wizard of Oz – to help illustrate this idea. We ask people to consider their voice as being a bit like the Wizard. If you remember the film, he first appears as a large green, ghostly head, surrounded by fire and smoke, who speaks in an angry booming voice and claims to be "great and powerful". However, at one point in the film, Dorothy's dog Toto discovers that the Wizard is actually being operated by a little man behind a curtain with various buttons and controls. When he realises that he's been spotted, the booming voice of the Wizard says: "Pay no attention to that man behind the curtain". Behind a frightening, mysterious exterior was something very vulnerable – but also something very relatable who could be understood. Ultimately, Dorothy and friends engage with the Wizard and in doing so gain new strength and knowledge for their journey ahead. In the long term, understanding the vulnerability that lies behind our own mental "curtains" gives us the chance to make peace with it and finally move on in our lives feeling stronger and more peaceful. But drawing back the curtain can be scary and challenging, and that is what our Compassionate Self can help us with. When the time comes, it will be stood right there beside us; helping us to pull back the curtain and engage with whatever is behind it.

So, with voices, we can ask ourselves questions like:

What's behind the curtain of our voices?
If we looked behind the curtain of our voice, is there a part that is maybe more vulnerable? A part that is being protected by the voice? Or maybe the voice is masking something that does not want to be seen? Or is not yet ready to be seen?

– Extract from CFT for Psychosis Manual [27]

In diagram C in the practical box, we introduce the Compassionate Self into the map. For many of us, this will be a new character (or self-identity) that we are bringing in and getting to know as we read through the pages of this book (especially in Chapter 4). The Compassionate Self is trained and developed so that it can help with the other relationships in the map. For example, the Compassionate Self can become the place from where these other relationships are organised and approached. In diagram D, the Compassionate Self is shown as being in the centre of a semi-circle – this represents its motivation to give equal attention and care to all the other parts and voices. One of us (Charlie) used to see someone in CFT therapy who referred to their Compassionate Self as "the conductor of the orchestra".

The Compassionate Self can help to resolve conflicts between the other parts and support them to work together in a more united, collaborative way. The overall aim here is for more *integration*; however, we need to be careful with what we mean when we use this word. We don't want integration to mean that all the various parts and voices become rolled up into one. As human beings we are all a collection of multiple selves – that is our nature, and that's the way it should be. For example, all of us have an angry self and a fearful self, and they are both helpful and useful in our everyday lives. Without angry self we couldn't stand up for our rights and with no fearful self we'd struggle to make decisions about genuine risks and dangers. However, while we don't want to get rid of them, we also don't want them to have an over-sized influence and take too much control. Instead, we want them to be an equal part of the whole team.

The American author, Dan Siegal, gives a very helpful example of this by suggesting that when we talk about integration, we should think of the process as being more like a *fruit salad* than a *smoothie*. In other words, maintaining separation between the different parts of ourselves (like the parts in a fruit salad) rather than blending them all together (like in a smoothie). In diagram D, you can see that this is how we've drawn the relationships: each of the parts and voices is still separate, but at the same time, are being helped to unite (to be "integrated") by the Compassionate Self. In this sense, the Compassionate Self is acting a bit like the fruit bowl – it's holding the fruit salad together.

Integration – as in fruit salad, not smoothie

Practices for compassionate relating to voices

There are several methods that you can use to practice relating to your voices in a more compassionate way. Some of these are verbal (relating in the form of words, such as talking or writing to them) and others are non-verbal (involving other aspects of communication, such as body-language, tone, and mental imagery). In this section we will focus on three specific techniques that in our experience have proved to be most helpful for people, which are relating to voices using 1) *role-play and acting/embodiment techniques*, 2) *imagery*, and 3) *letter-writing*.

1) Relating to voices using role-play and acting/ embodiment techniques

To start with, we can prepare for role-play techniques by bringing our visual map *to life*. Imagine that you are a set-designer, and you are now arranging the characters from your map onto a film set. One way of doing this might be to lay out some chairs or cushions around the room to represent each of the parts and voices on your map. Using chairs or cushions is helpful because then you can physically move around and sit down when taking the role of each character. If you don't have chairs and cushions, then it's fine to lay out pieces of paper as placemarks to sit or stand on, maybe with the name or description of each voice/part written down.

The idea of role-play is that we are really trying to bring our physical body into this process. It is a way of helping us connect with the emotional and motivational systems underlying each role (the same systems we described in Chapter 1). We've already got our map (practical box given earlier) and we are now bringing it to life. One example of a role play might be to begin with taking the role of a critical voice and speaking from that role (either as the voice, or as a spokesperson for the voice), and then to move over into the role of the Compassionate Self to respond to what the voice was saying. Don't worry if this doesn't make sense right now, because we'll be explaining it more as we go along.

When shifting between the chairs or placemarks, we are giving ourselves time and space to feel our way into each role. So, if our voice comes with feelings of frustration or anger, then we will be trying to connect with these feelings, postures, attitudes, and mindsets. It's the same as what an actor does: they really try to feel their way into the character's body. Think of some of the angry characters you've seen before in TV programmes or films. And now think about the actor who is playing that role. How do they do that? What is the process that the actor goes through to switch on this angry character when the director says "Action" and to switch it off again when they say "Cut"?

Actors really try to imagine what it would be like to be in the shoes – in the whole body – of that character. How would this character stand? How would they think? What would they do? What would it be like looking at the world through the eyes of this character? What body language, facial expressions, and voice tones would go with that? Importantly, the same is true with the Compassionate Self. When we shift over to this chair or placemark, we will allow plenty of time and space to connect with our soothing breathing, groundedness, and the particular qualities required to respond compassionately to this angry voice. In the character of the Compassionate Self, we would ask ourselves the question: "if I was being the most wise, courageous, and most compassionate version of myself, what would I say?" If this feels too difficult at the moment, you could also try imagining your ideal Compassionate Other instead. This could be a friend, a family member, a fictional character, or a historical figure – anyone who fits your idea of what compassion, courage, and kindness should look like.

> *[Stuart] tries to imagine what it would be like to step into this image and become this compassionate person. He walks around acting the part of his Compassionate Self, getting a sense of what that would feel like, how he would think, what he would do.*
>
> – Quote from "*Compassion for Voices*" film [29]

CHECK-IN BOX

How does that feel for you, this idea of acting and role-play? How does that feel being invited to play the role of a critical voice? And then responding to that in the role of your Compassionate Self?

Maybe you feel that you are still quite far away from your Compassionate Self? That's okay if you are. We hear this a lot: people feel that their Compassionate Self is quite unfamiliar to them, and that their "day-to-day" self feels very different to their Compassionate Self. Some people say that the Compassionate Self feels so far away that they worry they'll never be able to take that role.

Don't worry if it feels a bit fake, or if the things your Compassionate Self is doing and saying don't genuinely feel like how you usually relate to your voices. Don't worry if it feels a bit like "acting". It is! Actors do this all the time, and that's okay.

The only thing that matters here is considering giving this a go. Sometimes we have to start off by going through the motions first, and the feelings don't follow until later. You may have heard the expression: "Fake it till you make it!" and that's exactly what we're talking about here.

As well as role-playing how the Compassionate Self might respond to the angry voice, it might also be helpful to also think about what questions to ask the angry voice. For example, because the Compassionate Self generally wants to be helpful, it might want to understand the concerns of the angry voice a bit better in order to know how best to help.

I want to understand you. I want to help you feel safe.
— Quote from "*Compassion for Voices*" film [29]

Here are some examples of questions that the Compassionate Self might ask to try to better understand the angry voice, and some other things it might say to show understanding and validation towards the anger that the voice is holding:

Why are you angry? What would happen if you stopped or couldn't be angry? What would be your concern then?
That sounds really tough for you. I can see why you're frustrated. That makes a lot of sense.

Here are some more general suggestions for improving the relationship with voices, reproduced from an article that one of us (Eleanor) wrote with colleagues in 2017:

*   *Listen to what the voices have to say, but don't act on suggestions or commands.*
*   *Promote empathy between hearer and voice.*
*   *Curiosity:*
    *   *What is the voice concerned about?*
    *   *Is it trying to help in some way?*
    *   *What does the voice think would happen if you did x, and how would the voice feel after that?*

- *Recognizing the function the voice has and its capacity to help. Validate its effort, but suggest more useful or adaptive ways for the voice to help the person.*
- *Exploring shared resources and ways of moving forward.*

– From Moskowitz, Mosquera & Longden [44]

For example:

CRITICAL VOICE: "John is so weak. He always lets other people push him around. It's embarrassing."

COMPASSIONATE SELF: "It sounds like it really matters to you that John tries to stand up for himself."

CRITICAL VOICE: "Yes it does."

COMPASSIONATE SELF: "That must be hard work."

CRITICAL VOICE: "It is. I get tired of it."

COMPASSIONATE SELF: "Perhaps that's something I can help with. I notice that when you shout at John, it often makes him more afraid. I know John also wants to learn to stand up for himself, but at the moment it seems that neither of you are getting what you want."

CRITICAL VOICE: "I don't know. I suppose so."

COMPASSIONATE SELF: "I think there are ways of supporting John be more assertive that would be more effective – and also ways of responding to his fear that makes his problems worse. Let me tell you a bit about this, and we can find a way to solve this problem . . ."

The role-plays can take many different forms depending on the situation. Another thing that could be helpful when role-playing with voices is to also role-play the part or self that receives the anger or criticism from the voice. This part can have a chair or cushion too, and when we move into its role we can try and get into the feelings of what it is like being criticised, attacked, and bullied by the voice. Being in this role might involve us feeling quite small, defeated, and vulnerable. Here, our body language might be quite hunched or curled up. Our head might be down, and so on. You get the idea.

Playing the role of both the giver and receiver of the criticism can help us to really connect with the dominant-subordinate roles and mindsets that we talked about in Chapter 2. Once we have role-played this relationship, we can then move into the Compassionate Self as a "third" position, where it might take more of a reflective role. For example, the Compassionate Self might firstly observe and listen to the emotional conflict being played out between the voice and voice-hearer before responding to both parts with understanding and empathy for their concerns and for the conflict. The Compassionate Self might then offer some help for resolving the conflict, or for moving the relationship towards greater collaboration.

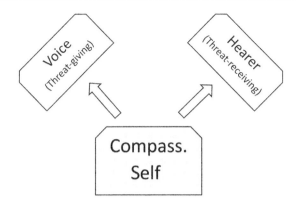

Chairs for voice-hearing relationship, and Compassionate Self

Given the many different scenarios that our Compassionate Self may be responding to, we also need it to be flexible in the type of qualities and approaches it uses. For instance, in some circumstances, the more gentle, warm, and nurturing qualities of compassion might be required. This might be true, for example, when the flow of compassion is directed to a part of ourselves that feels very scared and carries memory of a trauma. However, in other situations, it might be the stronger, more assertive, and courageous qualities that are required; for example, when first engaging with the hostility and attacks of an abusive voice, which requires strength and keeping composed. As we discussed previously, there is no single version of compassion. This is why the Compassionate Self needs to be wise and tuned in to the specific context of a situation, in order to know how to be most helpful. The motivation (*to be helpful and not harmful*) doesn't change, but the emotions and actions that go with that motivation will change depending on the situation.

Remember the example we gave in Chapter 4 that might work as a mantra or motto for the Compassionate Self:

> *May I be a person who is helpful to others.*
> *May I be helpful not harmful.*

In the appendices of this book, we have included a transcript of a conversation between a voice-hearer, Stuart, and his CFT therapist, where the therapist guides Stuart through a role-play exercise using two chairs: one chair for his voice and another for his Compassionate Self. If you like, you can use this transcript to do a practice role-play for yourself with another person. Maybe ask a friend, family member, or a mental health worker to read out the "therapist" parts of the transcript, while you read out the "Stuart" parts, and act it out together. Even though Stuart's voice-hearing experience is unlikely to match your own, it might still be helpful to role-play the script anyway to get a feel for what it is like to switch between chairs, and between the roles of voice and Compassionate Self. Remember, the more you practice these things, the more your mind and body get used to switching between patterns (from "threat mind" to "compassionate mind").

If you are interested to see some video demonstrations of the kinds of role-play techniques we've been describing in this section, the resource box gives details of a YouTube playlist that one of us (Charlie) has produced with two colleagues, Elisabeth Svanholmer and Rufus May. This is a collection of 15 demonstration videos that are freely available to watch in a playlist called *Engaging with Voices* [47].

RESOURCE BOX

VIDEO PLAYLIST: Engaging with Voices with Charlie, Rufus and Elisabeth

You can find the "Engaging with Voices" playlist on YouTube and on the webpage: www.relatingtovoices.com/videos

Video	Length
#1 Introducing ourselves, the videos, and our values	5:57
#2 Things to consider when you want to engage with voices	11:03
#3 Thinking about how to change the power balance	11:51
#4 Thinking about the function a voice might have	14:14
#5 How to work with nonverbal voices or voices that may not want to engage	9:44
#6 Mapping out voices in space	5:55
#7 Mapping out voices on paper	9:45
#8 Nurturing a Compassionate Self and encountering a voice	14:53
#9 Thinking about whether to talk directly or indirectly with a voice	5:33
#10 Talking to a voice from Compassionate Self	14:06
#11 Reflective practice with voices	12:08
#12 Talking to a voice that sounds like an abusive person from the past	3:01
#13 Writing with voices	7:02
#14 Talking with a voice can help understand its intentions	8:23
#15 Using the body	9:06

---

2) Relating to voices using imagery

Using imagery can be another way of (visually) representing voices and the relationships between them and us. It can also be a helpful tool for practicing new ways of relating to voices. Imagery might involve creating visualisations of what parts and voices look like as characters (e.g. with characteristics such as their facial expression, size, closeness to us, voice tone, and colours). These visual images can be helpful for understanding different aspects and intentions of voices. They can also provide opportunities for setting up safe, imagined situations in which the Compassionate Self might encounter the voice to begin a conversation. For example, in the next practical box, we guide you through an exercise where you are walking along the street and meet your voice coming towards you on the pavement. In other cases, you might prefer to meet your voice in the park, sitting down next to each other on a bench. Or instead, you might wish to meet your voice in the calm place you developed in Chapter 3.

With imagery/visualisations, the possibilities are endless. This is very helpful, because you can be creative in designing the scenarios which feel most suitable for you and the conversations that would be most useful to have. There may also be opportunities for you to gradually alter some of the voice's characteristics; for example, as the image of your voice receives compassion over time, there may be slight changes – perhaps a lightening of colour, a reduction of volume, or a gentler body language.

When we begin using imagery with voices, some of us can understandably find this very difficult. We might really struggle being in the presence of a voice's image because, for many of us, the presence of a voice can make us feel small and powerless. Of course, this is why in every CFT imagery practice we always start off with (yes, you guessed it!) activating and preparing our compassionate mind. However, if, at any point in the exercise, the presence of the voice starts to feel too overwhelming, then we always have choices. We don't have to keep focusing on the voice; we can instead bring our attention to the strength and calming qualities of the Compassionate Self. Or we can focus on our soothing breathing rhythm, or our calm place image. With imagery, there is always somewhere to go – we are never stuck or trapped. If anything feels too difficult, we can move to a different rung of our compassionate ladder (Chapter 4). When directing compassion towards something that is very difficult, there is no rush; these things take time. Please always take care of yourself while you're doing this.

PRACTICAL BOX

EXERCISE: Compassionate engagement with a voice using imagery*

In this exercise, we will be using imagery to set up a meeting between a voice and our Compassionate Self. The following is the script for a guided imagery practice. There are a few ways you can do this. You can either listen to our pre-recorded version of this script (uploaded on the website www. relatingtovoices.com/audios), or you can ask someone else to record a new version for you, or you can even record your own version. Either way, having an audio-recorded guide will be helpful, so that you can close your eyes and really focus on the images you are creating in your mind.

Once you have the recording ready, it might be helpful to quickly remind yourself about what you've learnt so far around the function of your voice, using the information you developed in the previous chapter. For example, you might have discovered that some voices have a role in signalling potential threats to you. Keeping the *function* in mind might just help you prepare for the kind of position to take when engaging with the voice. You may even prepare a few words, for example, "I know you're trying to help me and keep me safe by pointing out that I need to improve, but the way you criticise me and put me down does not help because it makes me less confident".

Okay, so when you're ready, here is the script:

Sit in an upright and comfortable position. Spend a few moments doing your soothing rhythm breathing and adopting a friendly facial expression. Allow your breathing to slow a little, and gently rest your attention in the flow of your breathing. Stay with this for 60 seconds or so.

Bring to mind some of the qualities of your ideal Compassionate Self.

First, consider the quality of **caring motivation** . . . a deep desire to be kind, caring, and supportive in the world. Imagine having these qualities and how it would feel in your body . . . what would it be like looking through your eyes with the intention to be caring? Consider what your body posture would be like . . . what your facial expression would look like . . . what your voice tone would sound like. . .

Second, consider the quality of **wisdom** . . . you understand that we have "tricky brains" that we did not choose for ourselves and that were created over millions of years of evolution. Again, imagine how it would feel to look out through the eyes of your Compassionate Self . . . having a deep understanding of how hard life can be. Knowing that all humans face struggles throughout life which is not their fault.

Finally, consider the quality of **strength and courage** . . . and just notice how that feels in your body. How you would hold your body . . . how you would stand with a sense of confidence and strength.

So, holding onto these three qualities, imagine walking down a street as your ideal Compassionate Self as you embody them within you. Really notice how it feels inside of you . . . imagine how you would walk . . . what that feels like. You have a deep intention to be sensitive to suffering, a desire to try to be supportive and to reduce distress. Imagine being in the body of your Compassionate Self and looking out at the world through that compassionate lens.

Now, as you are walking along the street, imagine that there in front of you is the image of your voice. As your Compassionate Self, just see if you can look out at this voice with a deep kindness and a caring motivation towards it.

What does your Compassionate Self understand about your voice? Can it validate or have empathy for why it's there? For why it's been doing what it's doing? Consider this for a few moments, then see if your Compassionate Self can convey this to the image of your voice. Is there anything that the Compassionate Self would like to say to the voice? Is there anything the Compassionate Self would like to do for the voice? Maybe to help it or support it in some way, given what the Compassionate Self knows about the *function* of the voice?

If you find your Compassionate Self is becoming angry and getting into an argument with the voice (or otherwise, getting anxious in the presence of the voice), just imagine taking a step back. Remember the idea of the "ladder" (from Chapter 4) and tune back into your soothing breathing rhythm or calm place for a while. Slowly try and engage with the qualities of your Compassionate Self and, when you feel ready, bring yourself back to imagining the voice.

If trying to think about or relate to your voice feels a bit too much then that's okay; instead, it might be helpful to just focus on the Compassionate Self's quality of strength and courage, knowing that it can tolerate being in the presence of the voice.

Spend a couple more minutes thinking about the experience before ending the exercise.

―――――

You can hear the audio recording of this exercise on: www.relatingto voices.com/audios

If you need a bit of time to think about how this exercise made you feel, please take that time, and join us back here whenever you're ready.

With this imagery exercise, it might be interesting to notice if anything changes each time you practice. For example, does the image of the voice change? Does your Compassionate Self feel more grounded in the voice's presence? When walking down the street, do you feel any more confident about the encounter that you know is about to take place? If you practice for a while and find that no changes occur naturally over time, then maybe see if you can *introduce* some changes: for example, the next time you do this exercise, you might try and intentionally tweak aspects of the image of your voice (e.g. colour, sound, and shape).

3) Relating to voices using letter-writing

In compassionate letter-writing, we often write from the viewpoint of our Compassionate Self to a voice. This might involve bringing empathy and wisdom to how it developed and an acknowledgement of its (protective) role. However, different letters can be used for different purposes. Some letters might be focused on helping a person to make sense of their voices, while others might be focused on the intention of making peace with them. Some letters might be an opportunity to practice assertiveness in relation to our voices, whereas others might offer reassurance. However, compassionate letter writing does not always need to be directed towards voices. For instance, it might be helpful to write a compassionate letter to a part of us that is struggling with the criticism and threats *received from* a voice. There may also be letters that could be written to a future self: for example, with the opening sentence: *"if you are reading this, future self, it is probably because you are having a difficult time with your voices. . .".*

As with the imagery exercises, there are multiple possible versions of letters. So have a think about what type of letter would be most helpful for you around your voice-hearing experience. In the CFT approach, the only thing that all these letters have in common is that they will all be written from the perspective of a compassionate mind (either your Compassionate Self or your Compassionate Other). In this section, we will guide you through a letter written from the Compassionate Self directly to a voice. We thought this might be a helpful one to try first but remember that you are the person who understands your experience best and we trust that your Compassionate Self will know better than us about how to start your practice of letter-writing.

In our experience of running a lot of letter-writing sessions with both voice-hearers and mental health workers, it is common for people to expect this to be difficult, or to find it tricky to start off with, only to then surprise themselves that they managed to get into quite a good writing flow. So, our advice would be to give yourself plenty to time to ease yourself into it. Maybe something like 10 minutes should be okay to begin with. Please don't worry about spelling or grammar or neatness – this is not the time for "perfection"! Try and just go with the flow.

Another thing that people sometimes notice is that their letter starts off compassionately, but then later can start veering towards a more critical or defensive tone. It you notice this, just tell yourself something like *"that's okay, it's understandable, it's not my fault"*, then take the opportunity to have a deep breath, ground yourself, and re-set with the motives and qualities of the Compassionate Self.

PRACTICAL BOX

EXERCISE: Writing a compassionate letter to a voice

As always in CFT, we engage our compassionate mind first. This involves connecting with the part of you that is going to write the letter – your Compassionate Self. We can prepare by setting our compassionate intention and motivation to what, and why, we are writing.

The following is a four-part guide that might be helpful in planning how to structure your letter. The first three parts are all aspects of compassionate *engagement* (identification, tuning in, and understanding), and the fourth part is making a plan for compassionate *action*.

Once you have read the guidance, you can use the space after to write your letter, from your Compassionate Self to your voice.

1. Identification

You can start the letter with a descriptive statement of what's been happening to help identify what it is that you'll be focusing on. This could be something specific that the voice has been saying to you, or a style with which the voice has been relating to you.

> *"Dear [voice],*
> *You have been very active over the last few days, criticising me a lot and calling me 'useless' and 'pathetic'. You were particularly loud and critical on Tuesday, after my sister came round for coffee, and you ended up just shouting at me again for three hours".*

2. Tuning in

You can then start focusing in on what emotions might be *behind* the voice, and the words of the voice. Again, this is a description, but this time it is connecting more with the emotions the voice is expressing.

> *"It sounds like you are frustrated, and you are feeling anger towards me. It feels like you have been particularly angry whenever I have had plans to do things or see people, and also when I don't stick up for myself."*

3. Understanding

Now the Compassionate Self can start engaging with the possible functions of the voice, being empathic, and acknowledging the voice's emotions and concerns.

> *"It is understandable why you are frustrated. You don't want me to be weak, because you are afraid that if I am then I'll get hurt. You want me to be stronger because you know how dangerous the world is. You want to protect me and keep me alert to all these threats out there – I get it, and I want that too".*

4. Action

Having focused a lot on engagement in the previous sections, the Compassionate Self can now move towards a commitment to creating change that is more action-focused. This might involve identifying areas in which you and your voices can work together towards your shared goals. However, it might also involve being assertive with the voice in some areas where the voice may be trying to help but is going about it in a way that is quite unhelpful.

"I understand why you feel you need to criticise me, but I think I would do better and be more likely to build up my strength if you didn't call me 'useless' all the time and if you were a bit more supportive of what I am doing, and the plans I am making. I want to be more confident too, the same as what you want, and I am working on it. For one, I am reading this CFT book, which is helping me with this. I have really started working on myself, and I'm making positive changes in my life. Over the next few weeks, my plan is to take more steps, like starting up swimming again, and I am going to set boundaries with my sister. I would like it if we could get on board with this plan together, [voice], I think we both want the same thing, but have just been going about it in different ways".

Your compassionate letter:

Examples of compassionate relating to voices

Now that we have covered the main techniques which we think are helpful in relating compassionately to voices (role-play, imagery, and letter-writing), we will return to the four voice-hearers that we met in the previous chapter (Alan, Deepa, Kwame, and Emily). Given their different experiences with voices, and the different understandings they have about the *function* of voices, we will consider what differences there might be in compassionate relating to voices. For each person, we will just give you a quick reminder of their voice-hearing experience, and their function, so that you don't have to keep referring back to Chapter 6.

Alan

Alan is the 54-year-old man who communicates with the voices of spirits. In Chapter 6, we established that Alan's voice-hearing may be linked to his key threats/fears (external: *people are harmful and untrustworthy*; and internal: *sadness and loneliness*) that were carried forward in time from some of his difficult early experiences (*early loss of his mother under mysterious circumstances*; *his dad's secrets*; *the break-up of his relationship*). Alan developed an understanding that his voices may be protective in that they were keeping him alert to possible threats in the world while also protecting him from his own painful emotions. In the following response examples, Alan's Compassionate Self firstly brings understanding and empathy for these functions (engagement), before setting an intention for what he is doing, or can do, to help going forward (action).

Alan's compassionate responses.

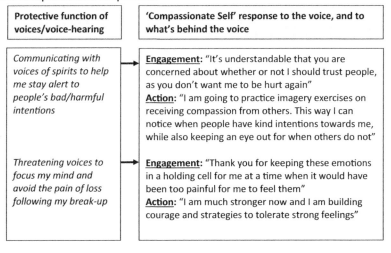

Protective function of voices/voice-hearing	'Compassionate Self' response to the voice, and to what's behind the voice
Communicating with voices of spirits to help me stay alert to people's bad/harmful intentions	**Engagement:** "It's understandable that you are concerned about whether or not I should trust people, as you don't want me to be hurt again" **Action:** "I am going to practice imagery exercises on receiving compassion from others. This way I can notice when people have kind intentions towards me, while also keeping an eye out for when others do not"
Threatening voices to focus my mind and avoid the pain of loss following my break-up	**Engagement:** "Thank you for keeping these emotions in a holding cell for me at a time when it would have been too painful for me to feel them" **Action:** "I am much stronger now and I am building courage and strategies to tolerate strong feelings"

Deepa

Deepa is the 32-year-old woman who hears the voices of her neighbours. In Chapter 6, we described how Deepa's voice-hearing may be linked to her key threats/fears (external: *people abandon me; people and institutions are out to harm me because of my race*; and internal: *shame "I'm a bad mother"; anger*) that were carried forward in time from some of her difficult early experiences (*abandoned by her birth mother and adopted; racial abuse; loss of her job and family*). Deepa's Compassionate Self starts off by bringing wisdom and understanding to the threat-based role of her voices, before setting an intention to help going forward.

Deepa's compassionate responses

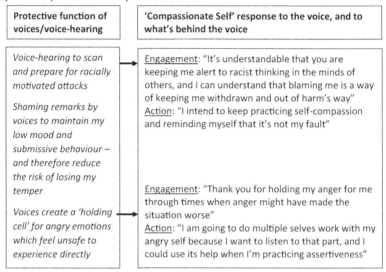

Protective function of voices/voice-hearing	'Compassionate Self' response to the voice, and to what's behind the voice
Voice-hearing to scan and prepare for racially motivated attacks *Shaming remarks by voices to maintain my low mood and submissive behaviour – and therefore reduce the risk of losing my temper*	Engagement: "It's understandable that you are keeping me alert to racist thinking in the minds of others, and I can understand that blaming me is a way of keeping me withdrawn and out of harm's way" Action: "I intend to keep practicing self-compassion and reminding myself that it's not my fault"
Voices create a 'holding cell' for angry emotions which feel unsafe to experience directly	Engagement: "Thank you for holding my anger for me through times when anger might have made the situation worse" Action: "I am going to do multiple selves work with my angry self because I want to listen to that part, and I could use its help when I'm practicing assertiveness"

Kwame

Kwame is the 40-year-old man who hears shaming voices that link to memories of his childhood sexual trauma. In Chapter 6, we established that Kwame's voice-hearing may be linked to his key threats/fears (external: *people are dangerous, harmful, abusive*; and internal: *overwhelming feelings; helplessness; his body responding to sexual abuse*) that were carried forward in time from his childhood trauma (*repeated sexual assault*). With these threat-based functions in mind, the responses of Kwame's Compassionate Self are very tuned in to the trauma memories that exist *behind the curtain* of the shaming voices. They are also very reaffirming of Kwame's strength and wisdom, updating the voices with what Kwame knows now (for example, that he is safe and that he does have control and choices over his life).

Kwame's compassionate responses

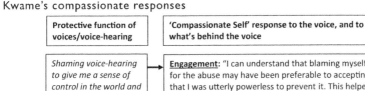

Protective function of voices/voice-hearing	'Compassionate Self' response to the voice, and to what's behind the voice
Shaming voice-hearing to give me a sense of control in the world and avoid helplessness: if I believe it's my fault, this means there are things I can do to prevent it from happening again	**Engagement:** "I can understand that blaming myself for the abuse may have been preferable to accepting that I was utterly powerless to prevent it. This helped me to feel more in control." **Action:** "Now that I am 40, I have learnt that I am safe and I have choices. I choose to not blame myself, but rather to blame the abusers. I have suffered enough and I will not let them make me suffer anymore"
Memory-based voices to draw my attention to unresolved childhood memories and feelings	**Engagement:** "Thank you for pointing out that there are memories that need my attention and care" **Action:** "I am working on processing my childhood trauma with my therapist. My therapist is helping me to bring my wise, strong, adult compassionate self into memory images involving my 10-year-old self"

Emily

Emily is the 27-year-old woman who hears voices of people talking in groups saying things about her like "mad" and "weirdo". In Chapter 6, we established that Emily's voice-hearing may be linked to her key threats/fears (external: *people are against me; groups are dangerous*; and internal: *I'm different; there's something wrong with me*) that were carried forward in time from her difficult experiences at school (*bullying*). In responding to the voices, Emily's Compassionate Self is focused on acknowledging their threat-based concerns and offering to work together in partnership with them to find a way of being more active and trying new things. So, not trying to get rid of the threat system, but instead bringing more of a balance between Emily's threat, soothing, and drive systems.

Emily's compassionate responses

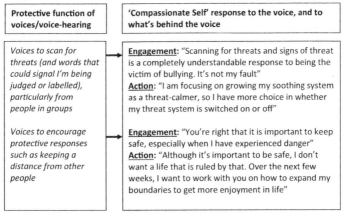

Protective function of voices/voice-hearing	'Compassionate Self' response to the voice, and to what's behind the voice
Voices to scan for threats (and words that could signal I'm being judged or labelled), particularly from people in groups	**Engagement:** "Scanning for threats and signs of threat is a completely understandable response to being the victim of bullying. It's not my fault" **Action:** "I am focusing on growing my soothing system as a threat-calmer, so I have more choice in whether my threat system is switched on or off"
Voices to encourage protective responses such as keeping a distance from other people	**Engagement:** "You're right that it is important to keep safe, especially when I have experienced danger" **Action:** "Although it's important to be safe, I don't want a life that is ruled by that. Over the next few weeks, I want to work with you on how to expand my boundaries to get more enjoyment in life"

Compassion for voices that do not have an identified (or identifiable) function

In these examples, all four people had identified possible functions for their voices (in Chapter 6). However, some of us will hear voices that do not appear to have a specific function (or perhaps we have not yet had a chance to explore what it is). Because of this, we wanted to offer some ideas for compassionate responses that do not rely on having any particular understanding of why the voice is there. In this case, we can just focus on the emotions being expressed, even if we don't know what might be behind them. If you find this difficult then it might help to imagine how you would respond to a real-life person: for example, if they were feeling frustrated and angry, what might you say to them to calm things down? Or what would you find helpful for someone to say to you?

Other examples of compassionate responses

"Compassionate Self" responses where there is no specific, or identified, function of voices

1) Compassionate focus towards the voice

Helping with the emotion detected in the voice
"You sound frustrated. Is there anything I can do to help with this?"

"I'm sorry you don't want us to leave the house; it's awful to feel afraid. I want to think of some ways to help us feel safer".

"You seem very angry. Did something particular happen today to upset you?"

"Is there anything you need from me right now?"

Compassionate assertiveness/boundary-setting with voice:
"It sounds like you have something to say that you feel is important. Now is not a good time as I'm about to go out, so how about we dedicate some time later at 7pm to really listen carefully to what is concerning you?"

"I want to understand your perspective, but I can't do that when you shout at me. I'm going to take a moment to settle down myself, then let's try to discuss things more calmly."

"I know you don't want me to go to this appointment but it's important I don't miss it. How about I describe what I expect is going to happen, then we can address any worries you might have."

2) Compassionate focus towards the part of me that's receiving the voice

Helping with the emotion experienced within the voice-hearer
"You know that feeling you have in your body when you are being insulted by the voice. Where is that? What does that feel like? I want to help you with that feeling. What does your body need right now?" (e.g. Strength? Grounding? A hug? And then, depending on what is identified, focusing on directing that towards yourself in order to meet that need).

3) Compassionate focus towards both (voice and voice-hearer relationship)

Helping with the relationship conflict
"I can see you are in a conflict here and it's getting very heated. Let's just all slow down a minute and do one of our grounding practices. Let's just notice the body, our posture, and our breathing rhythm for a minute. Stay with that. . . . And when things are more settled, we can come back to this."

Relating to your own voices with compassion

The final task of this chapter is to come up with a plan for some compassionate responses that apply to you and your voices. You might want to plan some responses that engage with specific functions of voices (similar to the previous examples), or you might want to plan some responses that are more general. Or perhaps you might want a mixture of both. In the first practical box, we have given three more examples of some compassionate responses linked to common functions of voices/voice-hearing. Each response has an element of compassionate engagement and compassionate action. There is then a blank box for you to write your own compassionate responses. Remember to refer back to the exercise we did in the previous chapter (page 123), where we explored some possible functions of your voices. In the second practical box, we have given some questions that might help you to come up with some compassionate responses to your voices, to yourself (the part hearing/receiving the voice) and to the voice and voice-hearer relationship in general.

PRACTICAL BOX

EXERCISE: Compassionate responses to your voices (with identified function)

Protective function of voices/voice-hearing	'Compassionate Self' response to the voice, and to what's behind the voice
Voice-hearing to set up protective responses	**Engagement:** "I know you're trying to help. Thank you for reminding me that I get scared, you're right I do" **Action:** "I want to start overcoming my fears now. I'm ready" *
Voice-hearing to focus my mind and avoid difficult feelings	**Engagement:** "It's understandable why you've been grabbing my attention and keeping my threat system active. It hasn't felt safe to be with emotions and memories that make me feel so vulnerable" **Action:** "Now that I'm practicing safeness and grounding, I'm finding the courage to explore difficult feelings, like sadness, that didn't feel safe before. In the long-term, this will help me resolve these feelings and they'll no longer have the power to trouble me in the same way."
Voices to 'hold' my disowned anger/rage	**Engagement:** "It's understandable why you've been holding my anger for me. Getting angry in the past didn't work and may have made the situation worse" **Action:** "I'm trying to re-connect with my angry self in therapy and am learning how to say 'no', and how to be assertive without being aggressive"

Protective function of voices/voice-hearing	'Compassionate Self' response to the voice, and to what's behind the voice
	Engagement: **Action:** **Engagement:** **Action:**

*Quote taken from the online video, "*Compassion for Voices: A tale of courage and hope*" [29]. URL link to video in references.

PRACTICAL BOX

EXERCISE: Compassionate responses (where there is no identified function)

1) Compassionate focus towards the voice

What emotion is the voice directing towards you?

Now write down a response that names this emotion (e.g. *it sounds like you are feeling X*), and then make some offers to help with this:

. . . .

. . . .

Would you like to set a boundary with your voice?

Write down a response that you feel fits with this emotion. For example, for an angry voice it might be firm but respectful, or comforting/reassuring for an anxious voice. This can acknowledge that while the voice has something important to communicate, your own needs are important too and this is why a boundary is needed (e.g. a set time or place that you can set aside for later to give the voice its opportunity to speak):

. . . .

. . . .

2) Compassionate focus towards the part that's *receiving* the voice

What feeling do you have in your body as the recipient of the voice?

Now write down a response that names this emotion (e.g. *this voice is making me feel X. This is located here in my body*), and then make some offers to help with this:

. . . .

. . . .

3) Compassionate focus towards both (voice and voice-hearer relationship)

Is there a conflict between you and the voice?

If your Compassionate Self could act as a peacekeeper (a third party who is coming in to help the two parts who are in conflict) what would it say or do to help? Think about how a marriage counsellor might address a fight between a wife and husband. Or how a referee de-escalates a conflict between opposing sports players or teams. What would you say to help switch from threat to calmness?

. . . .

. . . .

Once you have finished writing down your responses, we would encourage you to spend a bit of time practicing saying these out loud as your Compassionate Self. To do this, you can start off by getting into the right body posture, paying attention to your breathing rhythm, and to the qualities of your Compassionate Self (caring motivation, wisdom, and strength). Next, begin to focus on what the voice of the Compassionate Self would sound like: what sort of tone really helps to get across these compassionate qualities of strength and wisdom? Finally, practice reading out your compassionate responses in that same tone, doing your best to connect with the feelings behind the words.

As we've been saying throughout this book: remember to practice, practice, practice! Please don't be discouraged if you don't notice a positive difference straight away; this is very normal and to be expected, the same as when learning any new skill. However, practice really does pay off in the end. The psychologist K. Anders Ericsson [48], who studies the way people develop expertise, has some helpful advice here. He notes that the *type* of practice can be more important than the *amount*. So, it is better to do ten minutes of practice where you're really focusing on what you're doing and what you want to achieve than it is to do 30 minutes of half-hearted practice where you're not paying much attention. For example, imagine learning to play a new instrument. Less helpful practice would be just performing the same moves over again in a rather unfocussed, repetitive way. More productive practice would be thinking about what you hope to achieve and paying close attention to what works and what doesn't in order to get better each time. Dr. Ericsson refers to this as "deliberate" practice and, among other things, it involves actively checking in with what you are doing to help identify problems and solutions.

You can practice your compassionate stance and responses any time you like, from sitting in the living room, to standing in front of the mirror, to practicing in your head while you're brushing your teeth. Don't just wait for the voices to be around to practice your responses – that's often the hardest time to do it. It's much easier to practice when you're feeling calmer; and the more you practice, the more likely you'll be able to show up with your compassionate stance, voice tone, and intention towards your voices when you most need to. All the techniques that we discussed earlier in the chapter (role-play, imagery, and letter-writing) are essentially just different ways of practicing getting the flow of compassion going in and around the relationship with your voices. As you experiment with these things, you will find out which practices work better for you, and which not so well. There's no right or wrong here, it's just a question of discovering this for yourself and finding your own way along the compassionate path. We've both found our own ways with this, and it is a bumpy journey, full of trial and error, but we're glad we stayed with it. And we are now really grateful that we have the opportunity to help you with your journey too.

Time for a check in

We have certainly covered a lot in this chapter! How are you doing? There's a lot of information here and we wanted to finish by bringing the focus back to you. You are, after all, the most important person here; the person who we're writing this book for, and who we *really* want to help. So, we'd like to invite you to have a check-in with yourself. In the following box, there are four steps that can help to guide you through this:

1) Check in from the balcony
2) How am I feeling? How are my voices feeling?
3) Focus on the Compassionate Self
4) How can I direct compassion to these emotions/parts/voices?

This four-step check-in might be quite a useful one for you to use in your day-to-day life. A bit like the Flashcard we made in Chapter 5, this could be a good one to print out and take around with you as a reminder or prompt.

CHECK-IN BOX

1. Check in from the balcony

2. How am I feeling? How are my voices feeling?

Emotional selves/parts

....

....

Voices

....

....

3. Orientate to Compassionate Self

Caring motives
-self ↔ self
-self ↔ others

Wisdom
Strength
Courage

Engagement and action skills

Posture
Voice tone
Facial expression

Safeness & grounding
-parasympathetic nervous system
-calm threat
-prepare the mind

Role play
Method acting
Imagery
Memories

4. How can I direct compassion to these emotions/parts/voices?

Engagement
(it's understandable that... or
thank you for drawing my attention to...)

....

....

....

Action
(something I can do to help is...)

....

....

....

Final thoughts

Thank you for reading this book – and congratulations for sticking with it.

On page xii, we started off by noticing our shared intentions as both the readers and the authors of this book. We recognised that you had arrived here with a compassionate intention for "self-help" (doing something positive for yourself), and that we arrived here with a compassionate intention to offer something helpful for you. So, the fact that you have stuck with this book through to the end is really worth noting and celebrating. Just think, each time you picked up this book over the last few days, weeks, months, or even years, you have done so with a compassionate intention towards yourself. You have also done so with an intention to receive compassion from both of us, as in you've been open to *letting in* our help, and our desire to help you. And we are so very grateful for that, we really are. Each time you have thought about a new idea, or tried out an exercise, or stopped to notice how you are doing in a check-in box – these were all acts of giving and receiving compassion. I guess what we're saying is that: you've got this. Even if it may not feel like it at times, you know how to give and receive compassion.

In this final section, we wanted to provide a quick recap of the three parts we've covered. In Part 1, we thought about voice-hearing as a normal human experience and how different types of voices can be linked with different emotional systems. We also introduced Compassion Focused Therapy (CFT) and the evolutionary understandings about our "tricky brains" that inform the CFT approach. We noted that many millions of years of evolution has given us brains that are focused on threat, and which are more concerned with being "better safe than sorry" than whether we are feeling happy and peaceful in our lives. This can be distressing for all of us, but especially if have experienced threats and traumas, because it can make our brains have an even greater tendency to switch on these protective systems. Of course, none of this is our fault. It is just what happens when we have brains that evolved primarily for survival. However, we do have choices about how we can start training and shaping our brains in ways that can reduce distress and improve well-being, which is where CFT comes in.

In Part 2, we started the journey of how achieve this, beginning with creating safeness in our body and in our environment, and then by developing a Compassionate Self which can be trained and practiced. In Part 3, we then put the

DOI: 10.4324/9781003166269-11

Compassionate Self to work, firstly in relation to ourselves and our emotions, and secondly in relation to our voices. The final two chapters went into detailed examples of compassionate understanding and relating to different types of voice-hearing. We saw that compassion for voices can be a general position, or it can be more tailored to voices that have a specific identified role or function in our lives.

Reading that summary might just be an opportunity for you to reflect on your experience of reading this book. Are there any bits that have felt particularly relevant to you? Any bits that you might want to refer back to in the future? Are there any bits that you might like to share or discuss with someone, maybe another voice-hearer you know, or a friend, family member, or mental health worker? Please also remember that if this book didn't feel useful for you, or if you couldn't relate to the ideas, then it's not your fault. There are so many things that you know about your own experience which we don't know, and we really hope to keep learning more from our readers about what is helpful and what's not. Please always remember that *you* are the expert of your own experience as well as the expert of what is most helpful and compassionate for you. Don't be discouraged if you still can't imagine how things will get better. Recovery with compassion is not a goal or an end point; it is an ongoing process that gradually gets stronger over time.

Moving forward, our hope is that you will find ways of taking your Compassionate Self out from the pages of this book and into your daily life. Because of this, we'd like to invite you to consider a few questions that might help you to imagine what that could actually look like:

- With your Compassionate Self as your inner support and guide for the future, how would you want to live? What life choices would you make?
- If your Compassionate Self was showing up more in your future life, what would that look like? What would be different about how you stand, move around, and interact with people?
- Going forward with your Compassionate Self at your side, how would you relate to yourself, to others, and to your voices?

It does take effort to continue growing and training our Compassionate Self, and there are several barriers we all face in bringing compassion into our lives. If you are finding this hard, don't be disheartened – that's what it's like for most of us, so welcome to our club! We are all humans with threat systems that can quickly switch our minds back into patterns focused on danger and protection. However, when this happens, we can bring our compassionate understanding to this – the wisdom that it's not our fault – and use the skills in this book to help us re-set our compassionate minds.

It can be particularly hard to do this on our own, and sometimes it is helpful to speak to others about this and ask for support. There are many therapists and mental health workers out there who are trained in CFT, so don't be afraid to ask for this specifically if you want to build on the ideas in this book. Even if you decide to talk to someone who is not trained in CFT, you can always show them this book and ask to work through some parts together. It might also be helpful to link up with peer-support groups for voice-hearers; or if there isn't a local group, perhaps consider setting one up (the Hearing Voices Network website has advice of how to do this). In Appendix 2, we have provided a list of some websites that can direct you towards different types of resources and help, whether it's information, exercises, peer-support groups, or therapy.

However, regardless of what's happening externally in our lives, compassion is always something we can *choose* to connect to within ourselves. It is something we can learn to carry inside us with each moment, with each struggle.

Whatever form your journey takes moving forward, we wish you all the peace, success, and compassion you deserve. And thank you once again for allowing us to be a small part of that process.

Charlie and Eleanor

Appendices

Appendix 1. Role play script

Example of voice-hearer, Stuart, doing "chair work" with his CFT therapist

Therapist	Okay Stuart, so as you know we've been doing a lot of work in our sessions on building and deepening your Compassionate Self, and we've decided that now might be a good time to start bringing this compassionate part of you into conversation with your voices. This might help us to understand the voices a bit more.
	One way that we can start this conversation is to use these three chairs here. Whichever chair you are sitting in will mean that you are speaking from the perspective of that part of you, or that voice. When you're sitting in this chair, you'll be speaking as your Compassionate Self, and then you can move around the different chairs to take each of the different perspectives.
	How does that sound?
Stuart	It sounds okay, but it might be quite difficult because I've never really spoken to my voices. I don't know what will happen.
Therapist	What do you think could happen? What would you be worried about?
Stuart	Well, they might get angry with me, particularly the voice that's always critical and picking on me anyway.
Therapist	So, you're not quite sure how the voices will react? You're thinking it could be quite a tough conversation? Yes, I think you're right, you are doing something different here, trying something new, which can be quite a scary idea.
	What qualities of your Compassionate Self do you think could be helpful with this?

Stuart	Well, definitely courage. And maybe something about dealing with the uncertainty. And staying calm?
Therapist	Yes, this is really where the strength and courage of the Compassionate Self will come in. So, we'll start with your Compassionate Self, and really spend time activating your safeness system like we've practiced. Then, after that, focusing on the quality of courage.
	So, you'll be starting from this place of safeness, calmness, and courage; and of course, this is always a place you can come back to if you're ever feeling worried, unsafe, or out of your depth. You can just come back to this chair whenever you like, and we can do some soothing breathing, bringing you back to these feelings of calmness and safeness. Does that sound okay?
Stuart	Yes. It's good to know I've got somewhere to come back to.
Therapist	Okay, so shall we just think about which voice or voices you would like to have in the other chairs. Who is the Compassionate Self going to talk to?
Stuart	I guess the main voice that always nags me and says I'm useless and weak. I could speak to him and see what he has to say.
Therapist	Yes okay. So, that sounds like quite a critical male voice. Does he have a name, or is there some description we can use to identify him in the exercise?
Stuart	Yeah, I haven't thought about his name, but yeah we could call him something.
Therapist	What would you like to call him? Maybe either a name that sums up his character, or just a description like "critical voice"?
Stuart	I'd say probably Raven. For me, that's sort of a dark name.
Therapist	Okay, so we'll call your main critical voice Raven. Which chair do you want to be Raven's chair?
Stuart	That one [pointing].
Therapist	Okay. And are there are other voices that you'd also like to give a chair to, so that they can join in the conversation as well?
Stuart	There are other voices, but maybe it's too much to talk to everyone right now. I'd rather just focus on one. Raven is really the one that's there the most.

An option at this point would be to set up a third chair for the part of Stuart that responds to/receives the criticism from Raven. We would then get the interaction between Raven, and the internal response to hearing him, before shifting to the compassion chair and having the Compassionate Self relate to both the part of Stuart that experienced the attack, and to the voice of Raven itself. For example:

Therapist	Yes okay, good idea, so let's just have the Compassionate Self in this chair and Raven in this chair.
	Now in this third chair here, it might be helpful to have the part of you that receives this criticism from Raven. This is the part representing how you feel in response to Raven calling you useless and weak. How would you describe this part of you?
Stuart	This part of me feels beaten down and hurt. This part is quite scared of Raven's power, and of what he might do.
Therapist	Okay, so what would be the main feeling experienced by this part? For example, would it be feeling powerless, anxious. . . ?
Stuart	Yes, mainly anxious.
Therapist	Okay, so maybe we can either call this your "anxious part" or "anxious self". Or would you like to give this part a name as well?
Stuart	I'll call it my anxious self.
Therapist	Okay, we now have all the chairs full – one for Raven, one for your anxious self, and one for your Compassionate Self.
	Are you ready to start?

But in the current exercise, we'll stick to two chairs, with Compassionate Self directly questioning the voice . . .

Therapist	Yes okay, good idea. Let's just have the Compassionate Self in this chair and Raven in this chair.
	Okay Stuart, we'll now start with Compassionate Self. Just take a moment to close your eyes and touch base with your grounded body posture, your soothing breathing rhythm, then noticing your body slowing and calming. . .
	Now, begin becoming the Compassionate Self: focusing on qualities such as strength and caring-commitment, just like we discussed earlier.
	Compassionate Self is developing a curiosity and desire to understand Raven and why he is like he is. Compassionate Self wants to understand his views, his feelings, and why he speaks to you in such a critical way.

	Try to focus on the qualities you have as your Compassionate Self that can help you to talk to Raven to find out about some of these things.
	So, now just imagine that Raven, your critical voice, is sitting there in front of you in the other chair.
	Before you say anything, just take a minute to imagine what Raven looks like. Imagine his body posture, and the expression on his face.
	Imagine what Raven sounds like. Maybe imagine him saying some of the words that he frequently says to you. And think about what kinds of feelings he is directing towards you when he is saying these things.
	So, if you're ready, maybe just open your eyes. Now, still from the perspective of the Compassionate Self, just ask Raven whatever it is you want to ask him.
Stuart (as Compassionate Self [CS])	Why are you always telling me that I'm useless? What do you want?
Therapist	Okay thank you. So now if you move over to Raven's chair so that you can be a spokesman for Raven. And before you tell me Raven's answer, just take a moment to orientate to what it feels like to be Raven. Really try to get into what it feels like and where you experience these feelings in your body. The kinds of thoughts Raven has. How he acts, and how he holds his body. What sort of feelings are you having as Raven?
Stuart (as Raven)	I'm feeling annoyed, angry.
Therapist	Okay, so these are Raven's feeling's – annoyed and angry. And now I just want to repeat the question to Raven. If you could, please just tell me Raven's answer word for word. Raven, Stuart has asked you why you're always telling him that he's useless. He's wondering if there's a reason for this. Can you tell him what the reason is?
Stuart (as Raven)	I'm just telling the truth. You are useless. You're always messing things up.
Therapist	Okay, thank you Raven. And is there anything else you want to say to Stuart? Maybe about why you're angry?
Stuart (as Raven)	Yeah, well, if wasn't for me you'd be messing up even more. You're useless. That makes me angry. I need to keep telling you that so you get the message.

(Continued)

(Continued)

Therapist	Okay, thank you for your explanation Raven.
	So, Stuart, please can you now come back to the Compassionate Self's chair.
	Again, just take a moment to orientate to your Compassionate Self. What does your Compassionate Self notice?
Stuart (as CS)	Raven's very angry. He's really trying to get this message across to me that I'm useless.
Therapist	Okay yes, and he's trying to tell you that over and over again. I wonder why that is?
Stuart (as CS)	I don't know. He didn't really say. I'll ask him.
Therapist	Yes, maybe you could ask him what he's trying to achieve by doing this, or what he is hoping will be the outcome? One way of finding that out might be to ask him what would happen if he didn't criticise you?
Stuart (as CS)	Okay, Raven. What do you think would happen if you didn't criticise me?
Therapist	Now move over to Raven's chair.
	What does Raven think will happen if he suddenly stopped criticising?
Stuart (as Raven)	You'd make a fool of yourself. Everyone would find out what an idiot you were.
Therapist	Thank you for explaining that, Raven.
	Stuart, please now come back to the Compassionate Self's chair.
	So, that's interesting. Raven thinks that he has to criticise you to stop you from making a fool of yourself. What do you make of that?
Stuart (as CS)	He might be trying to keep me safe in some way. He's trying to warn me or something.
Therapist	Yes, so although he's expressing a lot of anger and criticism, there may be some kind of warning underneath that. Or that he's trying to protect you in some way.
	What do you think Raven might need from you right now so that he doesn't always need to fear the worst?
Stuart (as CS)	Raven, I can look out for myself. I'm a stronger person now, I'm feeling more confident around people. Yes, I've also been worried about making a fool of myself in the past, and I will keep my eye on that, but things are different now. I think I've got a lot to offer, and I do want to start taking steps forward in my life.

Therapist	That's brilliant, thank you for that.
	So now would you like to come back to Raven's chair. Just give yourself a moment to orientate yourself to how it feels to be Raven.
	What sort of feelings are coming up for you as Raven?
Stuart (as Raven)	I'm feeling anxious, scared.
Therapist	Okay, so anxious and scared. And Raven, if that anxiety and feeling of being scared had words, what would they say?
Stuart (as Raven)	I'm worried that you'll get rid of me. That you won't need me anymore. Maybe things *are* different now, but what if things get bad again? What will happen if I'm not around?
Therapist	Thank you for that Raven.
	Stuart, if you can now please come back to the Compassionate Self's chair.
	Again, just take a moment to orientate your Compassionate Self.
	Okay, so it seems that in addition to Raven trying to protect you in some way, he is also worried that you might try to get rid of him. That you won't need him anymore. What does your Compassionate Self think about that?
Stuart (as CS)	I'm surprised really. Surprised that he is worried about *me* getting rid of him.
Therapist	So, you are surprised?
Stuart (as CS)	Yes. I mean for starters, I can't get rid of him, he is just part of me now. I don't have the power to get rid of him. And anyway, perhaps I do need him to keep me in check. I just wish he wasn't so nasty, so critical all the time.
Therapist	Do you feel anything else about what Raven has said?
Stuart (as CS)	I feel a bit sorry for him that he's obviously scared about me getting rid of him.
Therapist	And what impact does it have on you when Raven is nasty and critical all the time?
Stuart (as CS)	Well, it makes me more likely to make a fool of myself. It paralyses me because I feel so bad. I'm so focused on him telling me that I'm useless, that I'm more likely to screw things up.
Therapist	So, what might you need from Raven for him to do what he wants, to protect you from making a fool of yourself?

(Continued)

(Continued)

Stuart (as CS)	I guess, you know . . . just a bit of support. It's like that example you gave of the compassionate teacher. I understand he might need to point these things out, but not to attack me the whole time.
Therapist	Okay, so it sounds as if you feel you cannot get rid of Raven, and that perhaps you wouldn't want to because you feel you need him in some way too – but that you wish the way he tried to warn and protect you was a bit more supportive, not attacking you the whole time. I wonder whether it might be worth telling Raven this yourself?
Stuart (as CS)	Okay. Raven, I'm not going to get rid of you. I can't. And I don't want to – I understand why you feel you the need to criticise me . . . but I think I would do better, and would be more likely to listen to your warnings, if you didn't call me useless all the time and if you were a bit more supportive of what I do.
Therapist	Thank you for that. So now would you like to come back to Raven's chair. Just give yourself a moment to orientate yourself to how it feels to be Raven. What sort of feelings are coming up for you as Raven?
Stuart (as Raven)	I feel better actually. Still anxious, but much less so.
Therapist	So less anxious, that's good. What do you think it is that made the difference?
Stuart (as Raven)	Well, I'm pleased Stuart is not going to get rid of me.
Therapist	So, if you feel anxious about that again, and fall into the cycle of criticising Stuart because you either feel worried that he'll make a fool of himself, or worried that he'll get rid of you, what would you need Stuart to say to you?
Stuart (as Raven)	I guess just to reassure me that he's not going to get rid of me and that things are better now. And yeah, perhaps that being critical is not very helpful anyway.
Therapist	Thank you for that, Raven. So, Stuart, please can you now come back to the Compassionate Self's chair. Again, just take a moment to orientate yourself to your Compassionate Self. What does your Compassionate Self think about what Raven said and what he needs? Do you think you might be able to help with that?
Stuart (as CS)	Yes, I would like to be able to do that. It makes sense.

Therapist	And would you like to practice now *exactly* what you will say if Raven becomes critical again?
Stuart (as CS)	Raven, thank you for trying to protect me. You don't need to worry, I'm stronger now and things are better. I'm not going to get rid of you, I need you too, but it's not helpful when you criticise me.
Therapist	Thank you for that. How does that feel?
Stuart (as CS)	It feels good. I think I can do that. I'm going to try to say that every time Raven criticises me. . .

Other potential questions to ask voices (from Corstens, Longden & May, 2012) [45]

1. Who are you? Do you have a name?
2. How old are you?
3. What do you look like?
4. How are you feeling at the moment?
5. Does (*name of voice-hearer*) know you?
6. When did you come into (*name's*) life? What was your reason?
7. Did you have to do anything to look after (*name*)?
8. What do you want to achieve for (*name*)?
9. What's your role in (*name's*) life? Are you helping or causing problems?
10. What would happen to (*name*) if you weren't there?
11. How does (*name*) feel about you?
12. What is it like being in (*name's*) life?
13. Would you like to change anything in your relationship with (*name*)?
14. Do the other voices know about you? What do they think of you? Do they collaborate with you?
15. Is there anything you want to advise/suggest to (*name*)?

This role play script was adapted from an earlier script produced for a CFT workshop in 2015 by C. Heriot-Maitland & N. Keen

Appendix 2. Resource list

There are so many wonderful resource lists already out there for people who hear voices. So rather than creating yet another one here, we thought it would be more helpful to direct you to the websites that we have found most useful for guiding people towards the kinds of help and information that they are looking for:

- **Information and resources about voice-hearing**

Understanding Voices www. understanding voices.com	This is a website launched in 2019 by a project called "Hearing the Voice" at Durham University in the UK. It is packed with pages of information about living with voices, as well as about the different kinds of help that are available for voice-hearers.
Relating to Voices www.relatingto voices.com	This is a website we set up to accompany this book. We will keep building this over time, adding more exercises and audio recordings similar to those we've shared already in this book.

- **Hearing voices networks and groups**

Intervoice www.intervoice online.org	This international website connects people and networks in the Hearing Voices Movement and community. On this website, you can find all the links to the various national networks that bring together people who hear voices.

- **Compassion Focused Therapy (CFT)**

Compassionate Mind Foundation www.compassionat emind.co.uk	This is a charity that was set up by Professor Paul Gilbert and colleagues to co-ordinate the international developments and training in CFT.
Balanced Minds www.balanced minds.com	This is a specialist provider of CFT therapy services. Balanced Minds have therapy clinics in London and Edinburgh (UK), and a team of online therapists providing CFT for people in other parts of the world.
CFT Therapist Directory www. cfttherapist.com	This website is an international directory of CFT-interested therapists. It was developed by the Compassionate Mind Foundation to help bring together the international CFT community.

39. Heriot-Maitland, C., CFT for voice-hearing and delusions in psychosis, in *Compassion Focused Therapy in Clinical Practice*, G. Simos and P. Gilbert, Editors. 2022, London: Routledge.

40. Petrocchi, N., C. Ottaviani, and A. Couyoumdjian, Compassion at the mirror: Exposure to a mirror increases the efficacy of a self-compassion manipulation in enhancing soothing positive affect and heart rate variability. *The Journal of Positive Psychology*, 2017. **12**(6): p. 525–536.

41. Matos, M., et al., How one experiences and embodies compassionate mind training influences its effectiveness. *Mindfulness*, 2017. **9**(4): p. 1224–1235.

42. Carter, L., et al., The impact of causal explanations on outcome in people experiencing psychosis: A systematic review. *Clin Psychol Psychother*, 2017. **24**(2): p. 332–347.

43. Horowitz, M.J., Intrusive and repetitive thoughts after experimental stress. A summary. *Arch Gen Psychiatry*, 1975. **32**(11): p. 1457–1463.

44. Moskowitz, A., D. Mosquera, and E. Longden, Auditory verbal hallucinations and the differential diagnosis of schizophrenia and dissociative disorders: Historical, empirical and clinical perspectives. *European Journal of Trauma & Dissociation*, 2017. **1**(1): p. 37–46.

45. Corstens, D., E. Longden, and R. May, Talking with voices: Exploring what is expressed by the voices people hear. *Psychosis-Psychological Social and Integrative Approaches*, 2012. **4**(2): p. 95–104.

46. Romme, M. and S. Escher, *Making Sense of Voices: A Guide for Mental Health Professionals Working with Voice-hearers.(Includes interview supplement)*. 2000, London: Mind Publications.

47. Engaging with Voices. *Engaging with Voices with Charlie, Rufus and Elisabeth [online video]*. 2019 [cited 2021]. Available from: https://youtube.com/playlist?list=P LOP1SbuZkEPwWlsOdfnRr5ZDDgiTN6FE5.

48. Ericsson, K.A., R.T. Krampe, and C. Tesch-Römer, The role of deliberate practice in the acquisition of expert performance. *Psychological Review*, 1993. **100**(3): p. 363.

Index

Note: Page numbers in *italics* indicate a figure and page numbers in **bold** indicate a table on the corresponding page.

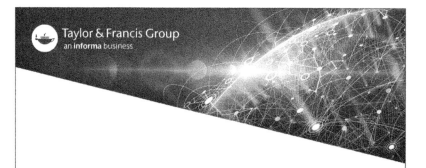